CONTEMPORARY
MUSIC EDUCATION

CONTEMPORARY MUSIC EDUCATION

Clifford K. Madsen
Florida State University

Terry Lee Kuhn
Kent State University

Harlan Davidson, Inc.
Arlington Heights, Illinois 60004

ISBN: 0-88295-350-8, paper

Library of Congress Card Number: 77-90672

Printed in the United States of America

92 91 90 89 6 7 8 9 10 MA

PREFACE

The focus of this text is teaching music in schools. It is written for education majors studying music as well as for music majors studying music techniques. The materials in this text are intended for a one-term course in music, possibly in combination with other texts. Undergraduate and graduate music majors may wish to use only Part I for discussions; those studying early childhood education or various therapeutic applications of music may be interested in the sequence of sample lessons in Part II.

Part I of the text is presented in question format, designed to elicit maximum discussion within a class, small group, or seminar. These questions derive from issues raised in actual classroom situations over a 10-year period. They are intended to stimulate thought as well as to elicit tentative solutions to problems involved in teaching today's students.

Part II of the text is extremely different from Part I. It presents previously tested sample lessons designed in a behavioral format. The lessons may be coordinated with Part I or used independently. The authors have found that, by alternating the material in the two parts, a student with little musical expertise is both intellectually challenged by answering the questions in Part I and is given a specific musical structure within a basic competency level for lessons presentation in

Part II. These lessons provide a specific detailed procedure for teaching, in contrast to the open-ended, thought-provoking questions contained in Part I. The lessons assume no previous musical expertise and can be taught at various grade levels according to the objectives of the teacher. Each sample lesson is intended to serve as a model and contains the music topic, behavioral objectives, and suggested procedures, as well as criteria for evaluation. Music specialists will, no doubt, augment these lessons with additional materials. Part III, an extensive resource guide, is included for this purpose.

The authors hope that this text will help teachers introduce their students to the world of music and that everyone will take enjoyment from the process.

Clifford K. Madsen
December 1977   *Terry Lee Kuhn*

Contents

ONE
TEACHING MUSIC—WHY ARE YOU HERE?

Paramount issues confronting today's teacher are often omitted from methods books. Many texts present material as though there were no difference between prospective teachers and the students they will be teaching. Perhaps this is why some textbooks seem to be less relevant than they might be to the student concerned with teaching, and more importantly, with personal preparation for life. The expression "preparation for life" need not be a meaningless cliché. To prepare college students for a relevant, useful life is often a focal point of goals and objectives. Today's student is concerned with how one fits into life's larger picture; the concern is specifically, "How do *I* relate?" Phrases such as "preparing the prospective teacher for life in a democracy" seem inadequate. Perhaps another phrase—"to stimulate thinking concerning life and the teaching profession"— would be better. However, with today's concern for specificity one needs to go even further. One might conjecture that college should teach a student *to live,* as evidenced by verbalizations demonstrating ability to analyze, criticize, and/or choose alternatives consistent with some value orientation; and to act, or behave consistently with one's verbalizations. Of course, prospective teachers also need to achieve competence in specific subject matter areas.

It would appear that those issues impinging directly upon students' life styles are the most crucial in their preparation for teaching. Some would state that in the preparation of teachers, subject matter should be the foremost consideration of the instructional endeavor. However, must not any undertaking first challenge, stimulate, and, in a word, *engage* the student?

We wish to caution the reader that questions that will be raised in Part I are extremely difficult; they are not questions with easy answers. Often a tentative answer appears wise. Sometimes no answer or even seemingly contradictory answers seem advisable. Regardless, we feel that easy questions, as well as their answers, can be looked up elsewhere. It is our hope that the student will develop a tolerance for ambiguity while proceeding through these pages *and* will begin to develop *personal* answers to the questions raised.

The student should be extremely critical while proceeding through these essays. Although many questions appear open-ended, the discriminating reader may uncover unwitting or even deliberate biases of the authors. For, as Socrates said: "Who knows how our most cherished beliefs became certainties with us and whether some secret wish did not furtively beget them, clothing desire in the dress of thought. There is no real knowledge until the mind turns round and examines itself."

Issues presented in this text start from the student outward and are primarily concerned with a student's personal lifestyle; that is, those issues that separate the "good" from the "real." There appear to be many sources that present "good" reasons for teaching: it is our hope that this text will help prospective teachers begin to develop personal answers to the real reasons for music teaching.

1
WHY SHALL WE TEACH?

WHY ARE YOU HERE?

Why are you here? A *good* answer might concern love for children, wanting each person to achieve his or her highest potential, or wanting to improve the human condition. Think for a moment about why you are *really* here preparing yourself to become a teacher. It appears that there is a *good* as well as a *real* reason for everything. If you do everything required of you for your degree and become a certified teacher, then will you have actually *failed* at everything in life that is really important to you? If you "have to teach," if you do not get the performance job you really want, if you have to work to put your spouse through school, if economics are bad and you have to cash in your "insurance policy" will you have failed if you actually end up doing that for which you are preparing yourself? Even if you eventually have to work, will you teach? If you become upset with these questions perhaps you should determine if you really want to become a teacher. If you were not here, where would you be? What would you be doing?

One good (real) reason for being in a university might be to find a husband or wife; however, finding a companion may be quite difficult if you spend too much time studying in the library, working on individual projects, or talking with your roommate. If the *real* reason for college is finding a spouse then perhaps one should do just that and not spend too much time with studies.

Another reason for attending college might be "just to learn." This reason seems "good"; yet a student may feel compelled to choose a major, decide on some aspect of education, then take no responsibility for learning teaching skills because "I am not going to be a teacher anyway." Is the reason still "good?" Real? Other students might set up questions that are not real and then play games with the process of deciding: "If I wanted to, could I?" or the reverse: "If I wanted to, I couldn't, could I?" or, "I can do anything I please" or, "I do not have to decide yet—how will I know if I like teaching until I try it?" Are "good" reasons and "real" reasons necessarily mutually exclusive? Must reasons be either-or? Could one "have to teach" and also be a good teacher, achieving pleasure in watching people learn?

Why should these questions be asked? It is because some people go to school only because it represents the path of least resistance. Many people go to school because their parents expect them to, because everyone they know is going, or because they become bored with another job. Others choose teaching because youngsters are not as threatening as adults. Some seem to not choose at all. Apparently, even though school is not what some prospective teachers want, they still *do* become teachers, discover that they do not like it, and become disenchanted, discouraged, or just bored.

In this situation everyone suffers: teachers and students. While it is indeed impossible for one to know precisely if one is going to like teaching, one's past behavior may provide a partial answer. To analyze past behavior begin by asking some basic questions: Do I enjoy learning? Do I spend time with children when I have the opportunity? Does it excite me to share a new idea? Do I find myself trying to teach others? Do I have some positive models in past teachers I can emulate? Have I ever been a successful scout leader, young people's leader or Sunday school teacher? Did I *enjoy* babysitting? Did I play "school" as a child? Am I positive with young people, especially younger siblings?

Why am I really here? Am I here in search of knowledge? Am I here in search of friendship? Am I here in search of love? Am I here in search of happiness? Am I here in search of tomorrow? Am I here in search of here? Am I here in search of myself? Questions must often be answered with other questions.

Why are you here?

WHY MORE THAN DESIRE?

Most of us *want* to be good teachers. Yet some prospective teachers verbalize only two aspects of teaching: (1) personal desire to be a good teacher, and (2) some "bad" teachers they do *not* want to emulate. Is wanting to enough? A great deal of research over the past several years indicates that there is a disparity between ideas and behaviors, between wanting to as opposed to actually doing.* How can one tell whether a student will be a good teacher? Is it possible to project future teaching effectiveness by analyzing what a student is doing now? A student may think: "I get to class about 70 percent of the time, but I'm going to be a 100 percent teacher," or, "I'm a C student, but I'm going to be an A teacher," or, "There are lots of ways to teach that I've heard about in my required classes, but I won't know what I'm going to do in the classroom until I get there."

Is there a relationship between being a good student and being a good teacher? Actually, what *is* being a good student? Is being a good student necessarily *making the grade*? Should a student spend time trying to relate to an insensitive professor when the student could be spending time in more productive ways? Can a student honestly depart from the academic "party-line" for the right reasons? Can a student have so full a life that the student will not tolerate mere busy work? Might a student complain about busy work yet actually be

*See Part III.

bored from time to time? How might a student assess personal honesty in learning?

Some students take four years to prepare themselves, and at the end are ill prepared. Perhaps they assume no relationship between what they *are* doing (learning) and what they *plan to do* (teaching). Yet one must face the possibility that thoughts expressing a disparity between preparing to teach and actual teaching may represent an "intellectual game." Suppose a basketball player were to say, "I really want to play basketball; however, I'm a little afraid to get up in front of all those people and I don't want to practice or think about it until the first real game. Practice as opposed to the real thing is really different you know." Is there the possibility that in the first game the player would be not only unprepared but also terrified?

You find yourself in this class reading this book at this particular institution in preparation to teach. Hundreds of others have gone before you. What happened to them? What happened to those people who have since graduated—*your* teachers—when they were students? Did they sit in classes like this one, preparing to do what you are preparing to do? Did they actually devise ways to be boring, insensitive, or difficult and unpleasant when they became your teachers? Did they say, "I want to be a bad teacher, I desire to teach poorly, or I choose to be insensitive—at least to some of my students." Think about some of your worst teachers. How did they become that way? Was it their desire—or did they want to be good teachers? What were they doing and how were they thinking as they progressed through classes such as this one? Wherein did they fail while others succeeded? Think about some of your best teachers. What makes the difference? Attitude? Desire? Effort? Would new instructional techniques have made the difference? Perhaps a good teacher does more than expected—perhaps a good student does also.

Why does it take more than desire?

WHY SHOULD YOU TEACH?

Many people enter teaching because they love children. Hopefully they have some experiences and knowledge they want to share with students. Perhaps you, reader, share this goal. That is, you want to acculturate students to share your values or perhaps to help each child develop optimum potential. Why are you entering the teaching profession? Were you drafted? Did somebody say—YOU! WE WANT YOU! *HERE,* IN THIS CLASSROOM! If you were not drafted, then presumably you choose to teach. In this sense you are preparing to impose, at least to some degree, society's values (that is, reading, writing, taking turns) on your students. Do you have a choice about making children's learning your business?

Do you believe that teaching means only relating facts to students or do you believe that values are also a part of the legitimate subject matter taught in school? Do you believe that even *deciding* what facts to present represents a value choice? Few people will get upset if you teach your students that Mozart (or a pop composer) wrote 41 symphonies (pop songs) because these are *facts;* however, what if you decided to teach them that Mozart (or a pop composer) wrote "great" music? At that point you are dealing with values.

It would appear that much of what is taught in schools concerns values, especially in music programs. Whether the teacher selects Mozart or a current popular song for the factual example also represents a value choice, at least to the degree that there is only so much time to spend in music presentations.

Some prospective teachers never fully realize the difference between (1) choosing to teach, and (2) choosing not to teach. The teacher who is not prepared to share (that is, to impose—if only by exclusion) because the teacher believes "students must develop their own values" has perhaps forgotten that even teaching children to establish their own values represents a value imposition by the teacher.

Another way to approach this question is to ask: Is knowledge happiness, or is ignorance bliss? It would appear that educators are committed to the idea that knowledge brings happiness and that people appreciate a subject in direct proportion to the experience and knowledge they have about that subject. Many educators derive their own happiness from teaching and very few would maintain that they can teach something they actually do not know. Yet even the knowledge of not knowing represents a kind of knowledge. In ignorance one is not even aware concerning those things about which one does not know. It would seem that only through diligent introspection and formal study can a student find individual answers to the problems of life. Thus, ignorance would not be bliss, but unconsciousness. It also appears that knowledge indeed provides happiness; that is, happiness ensues through exercising intelligence or learning. One may even be led to concur with Aristotle that the ultimate goal of life is happiness because we choose happiness for itself and never with a view to anything further; whereas, honor, pleasure, intellect, and service to others are chosen for the happiness they bring.

Many teachers feel that students need to pursue those paths which will make them most happy through their human relationships and through the effective use of their intelligence. That each student might prepare for a productive vocation and for worthwhile citizenship in the world community is another goal teachers have for their students. Intelligence concerning these things might be defined as analyzing, criticizing, and choosing alternatives consistent with some value orientation.

As a prospective teacher do you feel there are things about which you would not want to give your students a choice? That is, do you feel so strongly about some things that you are willing to impose them upon your students—because it is good for them? If you were not drafted into teaching—if you choose to teach—then what is it about which you feel so strongly? What do you want to share with your students? Which values will you impose? Will you impose some values you are not even aware you hold? Perhaps you believe that without certain knowledge your students' intelligence and future choice of life styles will be definitely impaired? Do you believe that particular parts of our culture (reading perhaps) *ought* to be passed on? Many great men of the past have imposed (taught) their values. Jesus elicited love from his disciples. Hitler attempted to impose the Aryan race on Germans. In a more ordinary sense most teachers just impose the "curriculum" on their students.

Why should you teach?

WHY MUSIC?

Why do people have music? Is it important? Is it necessary? Should music be required in the elementary and secondary school? Must all students participate? For how long? Will students be lacking if they do not experience and learn music? Why should we have music?

Such basic questions have long been asked in the history of institutional music, and many answers have been suggested in different societies concerning the functions of music. A simple overview might be useful: The *universality* of music has been noted; that is, music is found in all cultures. All cultures do not have the same kind of music, but all have music. To some, music is *communication*. If by communication one means a *reciprocal* interaction, then the term "communication" may be inadequate. Music communicates when it elicits a response. Is the elicitation one-way or two-way? This point suggests that universality may be intracultural but not intercultural. People from Western cultures do not have the same verbal language, yet they share enough of a common musical heritage that their responses to music are similar. Similar scale structures, instrumentation, harmony, rhythm, and melody are common to Western cultures. These are quite different from the musical elements of Eastern cultures.

Music in our society is often used for *personal expression,* both in listening and playing, for *understanding* and *enjoyment,* although many musicians do not relax in the presence of music, and for *socialization,* that is, to bring people together and to enhance interaction. If music did not exist would we be in this class? Music is something one can create, perform, listen to, and talk about. It can be used for *relaxation* as well as to change moods. Why else music?

Perhaps one answer to "Why music" revolves around the idea that music has always been a part of people's lives. In order for one to actually realize how important music is and what it does for us, music would have to be removed from one's culture. People are born into societies in which music is already present and they become accustomed to it. Is music a necessity to us when we have never been without it? Would we again make music if it were removed? Would music survive? Would we survive in the absence of music?

Do you know anyone who does not like music? Not just one type of music, but any or all music. There are very few people who do not respond to some type of music. It is probably safe to conjecture that music is an integral part of almost everyone's life; because every society has created its own music—and presumably enjoyed it.

Music seems to come naturally to younger children in their games and in their movements. Perhaps it ought to be encouraged even if only for the enjoyment and departure from the regular classroom routine. Music can stimulate qualities in students that otherwise might not show—voice, rhythm, humor, leadership, creativity. Music can give students a chance to develop while having fun. For the teacher, music can be another way to teach, to get to know the students, and to help students get to know each other.

Why music? For happiness. So that when people make knowledgeable choices from many types of music their lives can be enhanced. In every field there seems to be greater appreciation for excellence relative to one's knowledge of that field. Who can appreciate better a well-built house than a builder, or a fine timepiece than a watchmaker? The person who can analyze, criticize, and choose from many styles and pieces of music is more aware and therefore has the capacity for more happiness through music than the person who does not know yet "chooses" only one type of music. Perhaps music should also be a friend. As a friend music can provide company for many years. It can make you laugh when you are down, console you when you are lonely, and even comfort you when you are sick.

Why music?

2
WHOM SHALL WE TEACH?

WHO SELECTS?

What does it mean to select the curriculum? Are selectivity and censorship the same? Are they different? How should a teacher go about choosing those things the teacher believes students should know? Or, put another way, "What should the curriculum be? What if the teacher selects some learning activities and leaves out others? Is that censoring? Should a teacher choose experiences or activities that parents, principals, school board members, ministers, or newspaper editors think should not be available to students? Selecting and/or censoring obviously involves someone's choice. It is important to note that *while selecting makes choices available, censoring makes certain experiences or knowledge unavailable.* The important thing for the teacher to remember is that the *effects* of selecting and censoring are virtually identical on that group of people for whom the selection was made—especially if the students do not realize the choices involved. Many children are left with few choices, due either to effective selection or effective censoring by an authority. A teacher may select/censor as follows: "You may (must?) sing songs A, B, and C because they happen to be in our basal text, you may not sing song D because I do not know it. I also believe it is not good music worthy of being studied in school."

Selectivity and censorship present just such problems for the prospective teacher. Easy answers to problems concerning this dilemma might be, "I will let the students decide" or, "The curriculum is already determined by the school district." However, if any prospective teacher has just recently become aware of personal choices previously unknown, then that person will probably feel quite strongly concerning questions about who selects. Is there a certain kind of music about which you feel so deeply that you definitely want your students to either (a) be aware and knowledgeable about it, or (b) hopefully, not even know of its existence? To this degree, you, the teacher, might consider indoctrinating such knowledge in students. At this point is education the same as *indoctrination? To educate* is, perhaps, a milder word, but if the child's music experiences have been entirely determined, then the effect is the same.

What responsibility do you have to be knowledgeable of all kinds of music? What happens in the selection of music for elementary children? General music class? Chorus, band, or orchestra? For example, at Christmas time you have arranged a nice program of Christmas songs that you like and that your students perform well. Then two students come up to you after class and one says "Christmas is nice for you, but I'm Jewish. Do you know any Jewish songs?" The other student is a little black girl who wants to do a "soul rendition" of "Silent Night"—but you do not recognize the name of the artist she mentions. Who selects the music and, more importantly, ought it to be selected based on holidays, ethnic backgrounds, or only on the group's ability to perform it? Apparently, part of our common Western-Christian heritage includes Christmas music, Thanksgiving, Halloween, and patriotic songs. Should a more comprehensive heritage include Indian, Italian, and African music, rock, pop, classical—and perhaps, songs from the many excellent basal series? Might it include marches or orchestral and choral masterworks? What would you include?

Many educators would state that we should present all possible musics with good and bad examples of all styles so that students can learn and choose among these for themselves. Others might say, "Yes but I think the teacher should include only good examples of the best styles; after all, what is the teacher there for except to save the students' time by selecting the best of culture's experience?" However, what is "good" for one student may not be necessarily "good" for another. Some may want the teacher to select for students, perhaps even to censor the bulk of music that is available today. Others may want to provide maximum opportunities and expressions to allow students to select for themselves and not limit choices. Others might choose only that which students can perform easily.

The above considerations might be easier to resolve if it were not for the limitation of time. There is not enough *time* for the teacher to allow students to select or perform *all* available music. Even if there were no other restrictions the teacher would be forced to select or perhaps even censor just because of the small amount of teaching time. Some teachers resolve this question by stating that "At least my students will be exposed to what I think (value) is the best from all possible music." Yet what if this teacher can not name any pop tunes or performers? Maybe pop music does not even exist for this teacher. One might say that many of the children know "popular" music anyway since they get plenty of exposure to it from records, radio, and TV. However a counterposition maintains that students get exposure to "classical" music from those same sources—so that classical music might also be cut from the curriculum. Some music educators solve the problem by relying on lists of music selected by someone else. Even if students are exposed, does that mean they should not study that music formally?

Obviously, teachers must select, and, in doing so, perhaps teachers also censor. However, more important is the question: "Is this selection wrong?" If Christmas music were eliminated would that make the recorder or song flute program better? If some music from the basal series were eliminated, would that make other music better? If only easy instrumental or choral literature were performed, would that enhance other music experiences? These are questions that should be considered.

Some may feel that the value derived from students being allowed to make choices themselves is much more important than what music is presented or performed. Could one make the entire curriculum into a selectivity choice for the students? How might one go about this? From what music would the students choose? Since no one can choose that of which one is unaware, the student would have to draw from personal experiences. This seems very limiting. How would this apply to other subject matter areas? Should students choose everything—the books, the music, the time of day the class meets, the length of the lesson, the teacher, whether or not they learn music at all? How about reading, or arithmetic, or school at all? How much choice can students make? How much choice can teachers live with?

Many people would agree that teachers *should* select most of the curriculum for the students. If teachers and parents did not impose their values on students our entire society would become quite different. Would a new children-determined society represent an exciting improvement? Or something quite opposite? A way out of the decision dilemma for the prospective teacher might be not to consider choice and just to open whatever music is available and proceed. Thus, the decision has already been made. After that decision, by design or default, the teacher does not seem to have the problem. The teacher need not have to deal with current black music because there is none in the book. If 40 percent of the students in the room are black it still does not matter since there is no soul music in the book. Do teachers have an obligation to hear black music? Seek it out? Or perhaps just listen to the children talk about it? Should a teacher learn any music from other cultures or subcultures? Should the teacher permit textbooks, the principal, or the public to determine what values or choices are to be upheld in the music room? "But I told them they could sing any song in the book they wanted to. . . ." How much choice? And who decides how much choice? Are freedom and choice the same thing?

Perhaps one thing which ought be taught to all youngsters is the ability to make choices—if making choices is a value that the teacher selects for the curriculum.

Who selects?

WHO CAN CHOOSE?

Think of something that you want to teach your students: (a) How could you teach them so that they would believe but would also have a choice about believing? and (b) How could you teach them so that they would believe but would *not* have a choice about believing?

Did you choose to go to college? Not this particular college, but any college; that is, did you decide whether or not you would attend college at all? Did your parents ask, "Where do you want to go to college?" all the time *assuming* that you would go? Were you always expected to go to college? Did you always know you would? If so, how much choice did you have? Did your parents provide such bizarre and disparate choices as "Would you like to enter a convent, become an auto mechanic, or go to college?" Actually, how do people acquire the ability to choose? While growing up, parents, friends, teachers, and other contacts are very influential. How do these influences culminate at any certain time? Obviously, if a person does not know of something he cannot choose it. Try this: *Tell me something you do not know.*

One of the first levels of choice is knowledge, experienced vicariously or directly. Perhaps something could manifest itself randomly into one's life, but in that case one would not wittingly choose. It would seem that in order to choose something a person must have some experience with it. This experience can be either direct or vicarious. Direct experience is just that—direct. For example, concerning music one may hear or play some of it. One may experience it once, twice, or a hundred times; yet, at some point most people would agree that music had been directly experienced. Vicarious experience concerns those things which are learned in ways other than through direct experience. A child, after experiencing a certain kind of music could be taught about other kinds verbally. In the teaching process he could even be told that a certain composition is "better" than another. Much teaching exists on verbal levels. Thus, language provides opportunity for vicarious learning because of the many transfers that can be made from words, concepts, and ideas. This is particularly important in fields such as music where many aspects of form, theory, and style need to be transferred from one piece of music to another.

One could say that vicarious learning is not only important but represents the *future hope for our civilization.* Hopefully all students will not have to experience everything directly. Certainly we hope that a child does not need to participate in violence to learn that it is destructive, nor be prejudiced in order to learn about racial, religious, or sexual discrimination, nor engage in war to learn of desolation and death? Many things, because of their permanence or harmfulness, are better learned vicariously.

When is a choice real? Perhaps when some alternatives are distinctly achievable. However, when any outcome is sure from the beginning it is difficult to imagine how choice is involved. For instance, in some secondary classes "democracy" and "communism" are discussed as alternative forms of government. If alternatives were presented equally, would it then be surprising if some students chose communism? Does it appear to you that if everyone is given a choice, a real choice, that everyone would choose the same thing (that is, what they already believe)?

Think of something that you have believed all your life, and then determine to what extent you had a choice about believing it. If you have always believed something, then how could you have chosen it? *When* did you choose it if you always believed it? Did some experts rate all beliefs? On the basis of their ratings did you modify or change or improve your beliefs? If a child has a consistent censoring model, then the child will probably have no choice about personal behavior. If all a child ever experiences, observes, or is told about are kind human interactions, then will that child behave kindly —and not have a choice about it? Is this bad? Good?

Was there a time you did not believe something that you now believe? When you doubted something, try to remember how you thought about it. If you never doubted, ther did you have a choice? Define *doubt*. Is there a difference between saying something and having the words constitute reality: "I can fly to the moon if I want to. I choose not to. But not really. Not today. Not here." I may not have such a choice; that is, no choice is really involved. "I can jump from this fifth-story window if I want to. I have merely spoken the words. I would not, really, jump out the window."

Hopefully, by now you realize that if you believe in something, and if there has not been one instant or one second of your life in which you did *not* believe it, then you probably had no choice about it. Regardless of the verbal behavior it seems *logically impossible* to have and not to have a choice at the same time. When people once realize that they choose to do things, very few activities are left which *must* be done. If one believes that one *must* go to church, or school, or work, then that behavior does not represent a decision. It is not one of those things which are within one's control. Obviously, this is not necessarily the case; one does not *have* to go to church, or college, or major in music; one may deliberately *choose* to.

Think again of something that you want to teach your students to believe. How will you teach them so that they believe it and have a choice about believing it, or how will you teach them so that they believe it but do not have a choice about believing it? Are there some things about which you do not want your students to decide? Would you want your own child one day to come home from school in the first grade and say, "Teacher said that we get to choose whether or not we want to read and I decided not to." Do you want that? Or do you think that to read or not to read is far too important for the child to decide? Perhaps the teacher is waiting for the child to decide? It has been said that parents want their children to be free-thinking, independent individuals—but only after they graduate from college. How will you get students thinking? What if you do not believe your students have had a choice about certain important things? Do you have an obligation to teach them? Why do *you* want to change those students?

Some students *choose* to go to class. They make this choice every-day—and they generally miss more classes than most students. Some students *do not choose* to attend class. They do not think about it, they just attend every day. If you believed in something all your life perhaps you had no choice. Some students do not have a choice about class attendance. Skipping class is not a real alternative. Others actually choose every time whether or not to go to class. And the more one exercises that choice, what happens? The more classes one misses! Most people would agree that choice is "good" (a value) and that blind obedience is "bad."

One might ask other questions concerning choice: Why is this *our* town, *our* doctor, *our* team, *my* school? Is it by geographic association? Did we choose them? Did they choose us? In what way did we choose them? Do people who live in your university town begin to think that their town is good because they are there, or that they should decide certain things because they have lived there longer? How do they learn about the school and everything else that goes on at school? If you happen to be born in one part of the country you might be a Democrat or a Republican, just because you were born there—or Catholic or Protestant, or rich or poor. How do you know that those are the values that you *want* or *choose* or values that you just *have*? How do you, as a teacher, know which values ought to be perpetuated and which not? Suppose you are a teacher in a particular town. Many of your students are excited about a certain brand of clothes, a certain team, a strong tradition, or one type of music—obviously believing strongly that what they believe is indeed better. Does the situation determine the value? Should it? How does one determine what one *ought* to teach a student to like?

Some say that there are certain things about which people *ought not* be individually free to choose, because if they choose without regard for the rights of others then chaos would result. That is, society needs some form of order to exist. For this reason laws are established and enforced, rules of morality and protocols of etiquette are learned. Some may deviate from these to a certain degree, but no one can completely ignore them. In this respect, society as a whole chooses and individuals choose within a system.

Some might object to social systems that leave an individual with few "real" choices. Others might suggest that even though most people *can* choose, chances to use that ability are rare. It seems unfortunate that people occasionally narrow their field of choice from many alternatives to an either-or situation. For example, either-or demands dichotomy: a person is *either* working *or* not working. If one is not working then one is *either* in school *or* lazy. People also dichotomize morals: one is either honest or dishonest, either respectful or disrespectful, either patriot or traitor. Could it not be that many of these aspects actually exist along a continuum, rather than as dichotomous alternatives?

Do you hold any beliefs so strongly that you will indoctrinate them in students? A common view holds that each one of us should consider all points of view and then decide for oneself. This is repeatedly stated, yet is it really feasible? Do people who state it believe they are providing prospective teachers with something that is within the realm of possibility? How practical is that position? Specifically, one might ask: *What point of view about what?* For example, I know there exist over 2000 colleges. But I know more about some, and even more about a few others. Now, have I chosen what I believe concerning these institutions? If I *have* chosen, what was my field of choice? Did I pick my spouse from all possible people in the world? Is there a difference between having a real choice and merely saying the words? Does saying the words create the reality?

Who can choose?

WHO SHOULD PARTICIPATE?

The first time I remember feeling embarrassment, I must have been 7 or 8 years old. Some lady who knew us came up to me and my sisters. Looking at my younger sister the lady said, "Isn't she cute." Then she pointed to me and said in a somewhat unflattering tone, "Where did you get her? She doesn't look at all like the rest of you. She isn't one of *you*, is she?" These words made a lasting impression on me. To this day I feel embarrassed about showing my face in public and I guess that is also why I often feel that I am ugly, even though I know this isn't logical.

—from a college essay

Can these sorts of learnings be "taught" by well-meaning teachers in the classroom? Need the interaction even be as direct as the above encounter? Do children learn embarrassment not only through actual criticism, but also through tones of voice or facial expressions? Suppose that a young child sings a song and afterward his teacher says, "Oh, that was nice," while unconsciously making an unpleasant facial expression. What about the reactions of a child's classmates? Is participation in music activities at the elementary school level more important than the quality of performance? What do those students learn who are told to move their lips but not sing? How far should students be actively encouraged in band, chorus, and orchestra?

There are certain subjects in which people have a problem because they think they must have a great deal of talent just to participate. Unfortunately, music seems to be in this category. How many people sit around and worry about not being a good swimmer, saying, "I'm not going swimming because I'm not very good at it. I hate to swim with others because my form isn't too good." Most people are not overly concerned about how well they swim, talk, or drive a car. Yet, we have this fantastic thing called music—an experience to which practically everyone is responsive, a medium almost universal in its power to elicit reactions from people—and some say "I have *only* studied piano for 8 years! " Wow! Eight years! Others say, "I took band through high school—but quit." Do people say "I *only* finished college." Have you ever heard anyone apologize because he took "only" one year of chemistry and quit? Should people apologize because they do not end up in the concert hall, because they are not great writers, swimmers, or orators?

As a prospective elementary teacher how should you resolve the issue concerning participation and talent? How much should students participate in certain activities for reasons other than because they are good at that particular activity? Should students quit reading, writing, or speaking because they are not good at these things? Do we sometimes unwittingly teach students to feel that they are not good at certain activities such as music? If so, how is the feeling taught? You as a student may get up in front of the class to perform in a music activity and your stomach churns and you transmit a great deal of anxiety. Why? Did you ever have a teacher say, "You're off key" or "You have a bad voice"? How is it that a student learns embarrassment? Many classes have different level reading groups: the Robins, the Blue Jays, and the Buzzards. Every child seems to know which group is best. Students quickly learn that they are good —or bad—at the activity. So what should you do if you are bad at something—not participate? What if one is bad at life . . .? Hopefully *you* are not bad at living. Think about *talent* and *participation*. Obviously, the person with a lot of talent does not have a problem at the educational level.

If you are unzipped at a public function you really want people to tell you, but you do not like it very much. Criticism is necessary in every field and we do want to have it, but we generally do not *like* it. Criticism is even worse when it is undeserved. Can you think of a time in grade school when you got punished for something you did not do? Think how long it is that you have remembered it! That should tell us something. Were you upset over it? Did you think that the world was not fair? Why did it happen? Was it just a nasty old teacher? Or was that just a teacher who made a mistake—much like the rest of us? It is said that nothing is perceived so keenly nor felt as deeply as personal injustice.

Embarrassment. From where does it come? Some would say that it comes from inside; yet, not for the child, not initially. Someone always teaches it the first time. Or it can be learned vicariously by seeing someone else getting extreme disapproval. Think of two very little children taking off their clothes because it is sunny outside, and while they parade around the front lawn a mother comes out, blushes, and hurriedly dresses her youngster. The child learns quickly that "you better keep your clothes on or else something will be wrong." The first time embarrassment happens it does not come from within, but from without. The second or third time it may come from within. What about the second child who witnessed this? Did this youngster learn something too—vicariously?

Do music majors sometimes feel embarrassed? How do talented students find out they are talented, and how do the untalented ones find out that they are not talented? It seems that there should be a place for honest criticism, but "How soon?" and "At what level of development?" are the crucial questions. Schools of music do not need scores of music majors who are untalented; but then, public school music programs do not need performances that vie with those done by professional musicians either. Some people are not only embarrassed concerning musical talent: some are even embarrassed to talk in class. Where do students learn that embarrassment? How does it get inside? Have you ever watched people perform, doing a poor job, and felt embarrassed for them? Why? Most people believe that at some level talent and professional quality should make a difference. Most of us would not want to pay money to attend a symphony concert to hear music performed poorly. At the professional level one does not achieve distinction unless one has talent.

It has been suggested that people are embarrassed in musical activities because they are not trained or do not have enough talent. However, what about the well-trained, talented musician? Like any other expert, this person too can be embarrassed in certain situations. What if one is performing and accidentally plays a very noticeable wrong note. The performer is embarrassed because even with tremendous knowledge and skill the performer still made an error *before the audience.* Would the performer have been embarrassed if no audience had heard the mistake? Both the skilled and the unskilled suffer embarrassment at some time. Because our society values success so highly it is understandable that people feel ashamed when they do not "measure up."

As a partial answer to the participation question it might be suggested that every child should participate in as many things as possible until some age level. After that certain age or grade level, programs might be more specialized in order that those with greater abilities can continue (and perhaps those with more meagre talents, also). What should the level be? Middle grades? Junior high? Senior high? College? Graduate school? When should specialization begin? When do students learn that "they can't sing?" On the other hand, where do some students who want to be music majors while possessing only a modicum of talent learn that their talent justifies such specialization? (Could it be that at some point they should have been discouraged, but were not?) Hopefully, teachers can learn to give honest feedback to students without limiting any desire for experiences which enhance the choice of life's activities. It would seem that only a skilled and sensitive teacher can produce within each child a desire, founded on realism, to participate and enjoy.

Who should participate?

WHO IS RESPONSIBLE?

How much responsibility for learning ought to rest with the teacher and how much with the student? Some people blame their teachers when they are students, and then blame students when they become teachers for failures in the learning process. Yet, who is responsible for determining how much choice is available to students? Some teachers feel they are in the classroom to present the subject matter in the best possible way for learning, and that it is up to the students to decide whether or not they want to study and learn. Many of these teachers believe that students should not only take the responsibility for learning, but should share in decisions concerning what subjects should be taught. In this way they will learn to think for themselves and establish their own values. On the other hand, there are teachers who feel that most students are neither mature enough nor experienced enough to make such consequential decisions. According to this viewpoint, there are many important subjects that must be presented, and it is the teacher's responsibility to make every effort to see that the student learns the material being presented. Parents, too, are faced with these same conflicting philosophies of learning. They must decide whether to impinge their values upon their children, or teach their children to think and decide for themselves. Many parents provide choice, yet are not prepared to live with the results. Parents have been known to become extremely upset if their children change political allegiances, reject specific familial "taboos," or question religious beliefs and preferences while at college. Some students who find themselves at odds with parental values will avoid talking about these touchy subjects. Such a situation can estrange the family, promote indifference, and result in the progressive certainty that the other party "just doesn't understand. . . ."

Many teachers who recognize this parent-child dichotomy may fail to see the similarity between their own thinking and that of parents. The teacher must make a choice concerning student values: (1) a student can be encouraged to develop a personal set of values, or (2) a student can be expected to adopt the values of the teacher. The two possibilities are not necessarily inclusive; indeed, often they are mutually exclusive.

Many teachers, like parents, tacitly assume that students should share the same values that they hold. Perhaps only a few would openly admit this, yet their classroom performance betrays them and shows only indoctrination of their own values rather than teaching students to decide among alternatives. Most students adapt quite well to an authoritarian teacher in lieu of parents and learn very quickly to "play the game." Hours of student time are spent finding out what a teacher wants. The student learns that in order to succeed one must seek ways to please teachers.

Blatant flattery is insult; yet, when one observes a college "class discussion," where one student after another stands to testify to the teacher's viewpoint, it becomes apparent that college teachers may be the most naive species extant. If a student does not develop a personal set of values, may the reason be the insincerity fostered in just such a classroom situation where one cannot function honestly and examine values in an atmosphere of free exchange? It is a rare class indeed where a maverick student openly disagrees with a professor without some kind of reprisal. Reprisal may take the form of a patronizing facial expression, a caustic remark, or a defensive justification; in any case the student is made to understand that being a student permits one to make only the most innocuous innuendos of insurrection.

Possibly the most common example of unwittingly autocratic teaching is exemplified when a teacher deceives students and himself by stating, "There are many ways to approach this subject and there are divergent opinions concerning it." Then, conceding that this one way may not be the best, the teacher proceeds to narrow the field with one approach geared from only one viewpoint. It is foolish to suppose that a student can make a valid value judgment on any subject when knowledge is limited to one point of view. The problem is compounded when one realizes that because it has been said that "there are many ways to approach this subject," the student may actually think that a real decision has been made. One is reminded of the American who declares to the French chef that he has never tasted anything but American dishes, and "they are the best in the world."

The teacher, like the parent, has to decide whether the student should be given the responsibility and have the opportunity to establish individual values, or whether the student should be expected to subscribe to the values of the teacher. If the teacher decides that the student should develop his own set of values, *honest reciprocity* seems to be the most significant avenue toward this end.

Honest reciprocity demands sincerity and mutual respect. It is incongruous for a teacher to profess individual dignity and then treat students as inferiors. Many times just the tone of voice implies condescension. The teacher must start teaching students to approach teachers as individuals, not idols. Some teachers, even while engaging in dialogue, tend to keep the desk or podium in between, are concerned with titles and personal status, and rarely admit "I don't know." Ostensibly, this promotes respect, but the respect may be more in the mind of the teacher than in the student.

With honest reciprocity established the teacher and the student would then be fighting a common foe,—ignorance. The teacher would not need to impress the student with the teacher's intellectual or musical prowess (students are often extremely reinforcing). The student could move toward more and more independence and begin to understand that a different viewpoint will not alienate the teacher. Hopefully, the student would learn that personal views can be discussed honestly, and that the teacher was honestly trying to help the student to gain self understanding. When students, teachers, and parents can spend enough time to define issues, examine all possible evidence, and approach questions and ideas within a climate of honesty, then values can be established that consider the good of all concerned. This open reciprocal exchange tends to break down barriers of communication, and the teacher, as well as the student, benefits. This approach is becoming more and more prevalent within the classroom. Obviously, there will be many times when teachers and students will not agree and, at best, they may simply agree to disagree.

Regardless, if teachers actually believe that students should establish their own values, then they should teach in a manner conducive to this end and also *be prepared to accept the results!* The basic question remains: Is individual responsibility really a goal or just a misnomer for well-intended authoritarianism?

Who is responsible?

WHAT SHALL WE TEACH?

WHAT IS ACCULTURATION?

If you choose to teach from time to time you might be entrusted by society with two very broad yet mutually exclusive goals. One goal is to *acculturate,* that is, to make students aware of their cultural traditions and to instill the values of society without necessarily justifying them. The other goal is to innovate and lead the culture forward. Obviously, teaching toward these two goals simultaneously may provide some difficulties. Thus, the prospective teacher's job might be to make students aware of the traditions of the past, and aware of the culture in which they presently exist, while also teaching for the future.

The cultural heritage of the child is usually represented by standard subjects and is called the *curriculum*. As a prospective teacher you may believe certain things ought to be imposed. Which of society's values (social studies, music, mathematics, language arts, reading, creative arts) are you prepared to impose? Will you impose against the students' wishes? What specific geographical or political values ought to be passed on? For instance, if you take a job in a district where most of the people are against forced bussing to achieve racial or socio-economic balance, then is it your responsibility (perhaps even your duty) to teach your students (their children) the value system prevailing in the community? Or should you lead your students toward a different point of view—your own—or toward the viewpoint of others elsewhere?

You may think that you should lead students forward on a particular issue; that is, that you ought not to teach a value system inconsistent with your own. *But that may not be what this community hired you for.* Some teachers actually have been dismissed for leading students against community opinion on certain issues. Teachers have not been rehired because in part they found their jobs in jeopardy for teaching specific factual information. Yet, even factual information is sometimes not acceptable to some community members, especially if the factual information is viewed as "out of context" or intended "to incite and disrupt."

Is it your responsibility to acculturate the youth into the mainstream of the socialization process? What does society want? What do parents want? Do they want you to come into their community and radicalize their children? Will parents care if you teach their children to read—or will they expect you to? To spell? To write? To question? To criticize values? Perhaps to criticize their parents' values? What if you teach your students to be a little bit nicer to each other and from your point of view this means sharing, interacting, even touching. Yet being nice to one another in some social situations may mean "I'll be nice to those people as long as I do not have to be with them." Should you take a job if you believe in coming together and being close? Are you then violating the conscience of a particular part of that community with your values? When you take a teaching job you should realize that probably most parents expect you to make their little people just like themselves and perhaps a little smarter. You are entrusted with the acculturation of the child, to bring the student into the cultural mainstream. And what does that mean? It means that the student will share the basic values of parents, community, and nation.

Why do you as students sometimes upset your own parents when you go home for visits? It is because you change. Your values change.

Yet do most parents really want you to change? They may want you to do well in school, get good grades, engage in some innocuous extracurricular activities, but do they want you to change? Basically? Your ideas about religion, politics, and marriage? ("Don't come home and try to liberalize me, I'M YOUR FATHER!") On the other hand, you may want to teach because you want to change society, and perhaps some of you want to change society right down to its core. Thus, your curriculum might be a little bit radical. You might even try to select your job on the basis of values you hope to impose on students; you might wish to take a job where you can exercise your own curriculum. However, in that school perhaps the students do not need your values and your "curriculum" as much as do the students in the more "difficult" communities.

The greatest disillusionment for some teachers comes when they suddenly realize that a particular community *does not want* their values. This happens sometimes when teachers come from a "middle class" background and assume everyone shares their values. Alternately, a teacher may take a job in what is described as a "free school" and find that even some of the teachers there may not be very free. Perhaps, even without realizing it, teachers may be extremely regimented. We believe in freedom ("Don't do that!"). We believe in free access to materials, individualization ("Sit down, sit down"), and we also believe in self-actualization ("Mary, I told you once already"). And so on.

Socialization of children has always been a major goal of our society. In the past this was accomplished by the family. As society developed, the task was often relegated to the Church. Today the child is socialized by every form of organization the child is involved in—especially the school. Children come into contact with differing and often conflicting values, many of which are antithetical to those learned at home. While giving a child many different views on a subject may be good, inner stress and conflict can result when a child hears parents espousing one ideal and teachers another.

Many people agree that societal acculturation is not only good, but necessary. Children *ought* to learn reading, language arts, mathematics, and so on, because it is with these tools that children can eventually begin to broaden their own learning—with or without a teacher. This may also apply to such cultural values as honesty and patriotism. Why? Perhaps only because we tend to teach *what* and *as* we were taught. King Solomon said long ago that if one teaches a child with consistency throughout his youth, then he will not deviate from those ways as he grows older.

Given a dynamic culture such as our own, acculturation and innovation may not be compatible. Merely teaching a history lesson illustrates that times were not always as they are today—and that perhaps there are few aspects *inherently* right about one's culture. It may be that the goal of innovation is contingent on being aware of one's cultural heritage. Awareness of traditions, of the people who created them, and of events leading to prevailing values might help prepare the way for cultural innovation.

To a prospective teacher the real issue concerns what is meant by "innovation." *Innovation* might mean anything from indoctrinating students with one's own personal values (possibly radically opposed to those held by the community) to making students aware of change and the processes of change so that they may do their own innovating.

Some would say that the teacher's duty is to acculturate children, that is, "bringing them into their cultural tradition" so that they become functioning and contributing members of society. Additionally, children should be taught the dynamic nature of culture, opposing viewpoints, and the process of change. Further, some people feel that the teacher should not try to indoctrinate children to views possessed by the teacher which are contrary to what (they believe) the community, state, or nation believes. They believe that any teacher who has developed beliefs uncommon to society as a whole and who imposes those beliefs on youngsters assumes too much self-importance—thinking that one person should be the sole decider of what children learn.

How might one resolve these two conflicting goals: one goal to teach what is, and the other to teach what might be? Obviously, one can not do both at exactly the same time. You can not develop a new spelling system while you are teaching the old. You cannot free little girls from what you might consider undesirable male-female stereotypes while imposing those same stereotypes. Perhaps you can alternate, teaching the old for five minutes, then teaching the new, but you can not teach both simultaneously. If you are courageous and want to innovate and lead the culture forward you will be in good company; but, you should also be aware of the possible consequences. Socrates said "Woe to him who teaches men faster than they can learn." Socrates taught radically—and died for it. Jesus taught such radical lessons as the Sermon on the Mount. Martin Luther King spoke courageously, not radically, for nonviolent protest.

If you attempt to lead the culture forward too much, too fast, too soon, many things can happen. All the way from being disliked to outcast, harassed, and even dismissed.

What is acculturation?

WHAT IS OUR SUBJECT?

Our specific subject matter is music. Music involves numerous activities that people identify with the phenomenon of music: composition, performance, listening, musical discussion, aesthetic sensitivity and, indeed, any and every activity related to these. In other words, the subject of music includes anything that functions musically for people. Behaviorally, it may be stated that music may be *composed, performed, listened to, talked about,* and used for *extra-musical* purposes. All aspects are important to students and may be studied individually and/or collectively. Many texts concerning elementary music education advocate that the student experience all aspects of music within each lesson. That is, students should create, engage in rhythmic bodily activities, listen, discuss, read notation, and perform. Students in secondary education usually spend most of their time performing a variety of music materials. The subject matter of music may be experienced in many ways.

Composition includes all activities directed toward the creation of music. Such activities span from Beethoven creating a symphony to a child spontaneously answering a musical question with two notes. Composition is thought to include creativity relating to many aspects of music other than just composing songs; for instance, interpretation in performance, improvisation, and determining phrases.

Performance includes singing or playing an instrument. On the secondary and professional level audiences engage skilled musicians to perform; on the avocational level people play or sing in community groups for socialization or for personal pleasure. Many people perform to entertain themselves or to use up some of life's time. For all of these, musical performance involves developing neuro-muscular responses in relation to aural discriminations.

Listening concerns attending to musical performance; listening can lead to exposure to diverse musical styles and the development of discriminative listening skills. Many students are conditioned to passive listening—to being "bathed in sound"—yet most educators believe that listening should also include knowledge of musical elements. Listening might include discriminations concerning the way music is put together (theory and style) as well as aspects dealing with sophisticated aural discernments such as instrumentation, form, and rhythm. Listening may even include basic acoustics. Specific lessons in Part II are intended to provide models for increasing listening as well as performance and appreciation skills.

Musical *discussions* necessitate a vocabulary of musical terms and expressions which people can use to label and talk about the musical phenomena. Terms are needed to describe music occurring in time (the words are static while the music is temporal) and to allow communication of the effects music has on listeners. Most youngsters seem capable of talking about music in their own vocabulary, yet in a program designed to acquaint students with stylistic elements of music, more formal words are needed. The following two lists represent two of many disparate vocabularies concerning our subject matter:

Chant	Classical
Medieval	Country-Western
Renaissance	Movie
Baroque	Blue Grass
Rococo	Jazz
Classic	Rock
Romantic	Soul
Impressionistic	Gospel
Electronic	Folk
Modern	Musicals

Which of these two lists or, more importantly, what combinations do you consider to be most useful for presentation to students? Which of these lists or what alternatives would be most beneficial to your students? Why? From the viewpoint of society at large what music if any is most meaningful or most representative of our culture? Western society has produced the styles contained on both of the above lists. Is one list more "real" or "better than" the other list? The styles within each list could be ranked in order of importance to teacher, student, and society. It should be noted that the entire first list might be contained in the "Classical" category of the second list and the entire second list could be contained in the "Modern" category of the first list. The difference in emphasis is quite clear, yet there are many styles *not even listed.* We have pointed out that sometimes teachers have two contradictory goals. It appears that even within a single society some conflict of values might occur, depending on who one is and *what one values.*

Additionally, the vocabulary people use to talk about music often serves to differentiate rather than communicate similar goals and experiences. It should be remembered that perhaps music's meaning or significance is not at all dependent upon verbalizations. It seems wise for the prospective teacher to learn the many words various people may use to describe "their music." Music has been called a nonverbal language. It would be unfortunate if music failed to communicate only because of prejudices built solely upon words.

What is our subject?

WHAT IS EXTRA-MUSICAL?

If the subject matter of music learning consists of those activities in which music is composed, performed, listened to, and discussed, then extra-musical activities are those in which music occurs but not as the major element of subject matter. Some musicians object to using music other than for its own sake, yet such things as drawing to music, dancing, marching, moving to music, background music, industrial music, Muzak, and shopping center music are common examples of utilizing music as a secondary concern. In elementary grades the pantomiming of stories to music might be called an activity in the field of dramatics *and* music. Painting to music is probably an artistic *and* musical activity. On the secondary level participation in the marching band might be listed under many situations simultaneously.

Often in an attempt to make music meaningful to students, teachers rely on extra-musical associations. This may be an excellent way to approach the young child—if the child is already acculturated in the extra-musical aspects of the teaching process. The indirect, or extra-musical approach is preferable if the child relates to whatever the teacher is using to bring the child into the child's musical heritage— be it a bus to connote moving, a cow to connote longness (moooooooo), or a ladder to connote climbing. Any number of extra-musical referents can be used to connote moving, long, rising, and so on. If, however, the child is not so acculturated (that is, the child has not had previous experience with the extra-musical examples) then the teacher wastes time teaching an association that is not viable: cows are long (in music), buses move (in music), and ladders rise (in music). Does music do this too somehow? Extra-musical considerations might better be left to industry (to entice shoppers into the store, keep them there, and so on) than used as a vehicle to relate to children. Buses might be presented as vehicles of transportation, cows as animals which produce milk, and music as subject matter. At the secondary level music is generally thought to have social value outside the music experience *per se.* Even here care should be taken to differentiate musical from extra-musical considerations—there are many prison bands and choruses.

The tremendous power of music to enhance *other* activities, however, should not be underestimated. Music can help young fingers move freely over paper in creating abstract designs, it can provide thought associations in getting ideas, it can help in acquiring motor skills, it can evoke many moods (which have been previously learned), it can make periods of rest more interesting, and it can stimulate discussions about nearly any topic. Playing a Gregorian Chant may enhance study of life in the Middle Ages. Music can be used to help teach nationalism ("The Star Spangled Banner"), racism ("Society's Child"), poverty ("Tobacco Road"), or war ("Johnny Has Gone For A Soldier"). Music—like art—may reflect the conscience, values, attitudes, and history of society and perhaps can be used effectively in teaching other subject matters.

In some situations teachers may choose to use music as an effective reward to enhance other subject matter. In this case music may indeed prove of value not only for its own sake but as a helper to other subjects as well. Some children might work faster, or attend to a difficult exercise longer if they knew that an enjoyable music activity is contingent on their academic performance. Also, there is some evidence to indicate that developing music listening and performance skills may actually help the child make discriminations in language arts (for instance, to identify word sounds which are the same or different).

Some educators believe that it is good to use some subject matters to help teach or augment other subject matter; others do not. It does seem wise that the teacher make basic differentiations in order to know precisely what knowledge is being learned when various learning activities are combined. There are many people who believe that music should never be used for any purpose other than for its own sake.

Another very important issue dealing with subject matter concerns the relationship between the classroom teacher who teaches music and the music teacher (music specialist) who also teaches music. If both persons teach music to children, then cooperation between the two ought to be beneficial to their students. Sometimes the music specialist selects the primary learning experiences for the students and enlists the help of the classroom teacher to implement these goals. Sometimes curriculum decisions are made jointly. Often the degree of participation depends upon the interest of both teachers in cooperating with each other.

Often the music specialist implements the specific subject matter, that is, music experiences dealing with specific music goals, while the classroom teacher deals more with extra-musical activities. Sometimes there is not a music specialist available and the classroom teacher is the only person who will bring music to the children. In this case the total academic musical development of the child is determined by the regular classroom teacher. There are also other academic structures in which teachers share the responsibility for many children. In these situations it is usually the teacher who desires most that children have music who becomes the "music teacher." Regardless of who takes the responsibility, it seems important that cooperation as well as initiative be maintained to insure that the musical and extra-musical development of the student actually takes place. Indeed, "Man does not live by bread alone."

What is extra-musical?

WHAT IS CREATIVITY?

Is creativity a reorganization of past experience? Is one born with it? Or is it transcendental, mystical, and unexplainable in the real world? Can it be taught? Can it be learned? How might teaching creativity differ from learning creativity? These are questions which confront the prospective teacher.

If creativity cannot be learned, then examining other issues seems futile. If it can be taught but not learned or if it can be learned but not taught, the pursuit seems irrelevant. Only if creativity can be taught *and* learned need an educator be concerned with the situation in which such learning occurs. While many views of teaching do not dichotomize teaching and learning, if students can only create from "something" then what information and/or material does the student need? At what point in an activity might progressive instruction inhibit future creativity?

Is creativity a *process* or is it a product? Do we remember Beethoven because of the creative process through which he composed or because of his musical product? Do we remember artists for the process through which they go or because of the paintings they produce? When one thinks of an artist such as Picasso does one imagine his doing something or does one think of the several canvases upon which his brush was applied? Do we consider a person a creative cook because of many hours of activity involved in preparing a fine meal, or because of the tastiness of the meal itself? When we think of fine art we usually think of creativity as being a product; however, when we think of applying divergent solutions to life's daily problems we usually think of creativity as being an activity, a process.

Initially it would seem that creativity involves choice, at the verbal as well as the manipulative level—the selecting or putting together of materials and experiences. If a teacher specifies a *behavioral objective* which identifies the precise terminal behavior at the outset of a lesson, then how much creativity (choice) can a student display? Most teachers want students to be creative, yet how much instruction does it take even to get students started? Can a student start from absolutely nothing? Concerning verbal choosing most students select from things they are aware of; or, to state it in reverse, "I do not know any piece of music by Brahms and I do not like anything he wrote." If students are unaware of Brahms' music—that is, if Brahms' music does not exist for them—then they do not get to choose to have Brahms or not to have Brahms. They just do not know about Brahms and therefore have no choice, unless, of course, some of his music accidentally falls into their life. Again it should be stated that some people believe that if they say the words there is choice; therefore, if a teacher can get students to say "I do not like the music of Brahms" even if they do not know any of it, then they have "chosen."

What do people base their choices upon? Apparently most people base their choices either on their own experience or upon vicarious and/or haphazard experiences. If students need some instruction just to get started, then how much instruction does that take? How much teaching ought the teacher to do in manipulating materials? For example, if a teacher brought a square of clay in the classroom, left it there, and said nothing about it—how long would it take for students to find out what it was and what they could do with it? What would it take to get the students to manipulate it, to find out not only that it is malleable, but also that it is possible to make things with it? It appears that a certain amount of instruction is necessary just to get started and that more instruction is needed to stimulate the creative potential. However, progressive instruction may at some point inhibit creativity. Perhaps the reason many people are creative is because they received little or no formal instruction. Sometimes teachers *tell* their students to be creative ("You do not have to make what I am making. Make any kind of pot you choose!"), but do the words or the actions constitute the reality? Are students creative because teachers tell them to be? Perhaps we need to set up the conditions which nurture the development of those mental capacities which produce creative products and processes.

Questions which seem paramount as far as creativity is concerned are (1) How can we set up the conditions that foster creativity? (2)

What should be the evaluation of the creative effort and/or product? and (3) Who should evaluate it?

If teachers want to teach creativity to students, then should the creative product be evaluated, and, if so, by whom? Should teachers say, "That is grade 'B' creative," or should they say "Which one do you like best," or "Tell me about it?" Instead of saying, "Choose A, B, C, or All of the above," perhaps a teacher could ask "Why?" Some teachers try to solve the evaluation problem by being nondirective and nonspecific, that is, by saying that they like *everything* their students do. A child may work very hard on one painting and think that another one is terrible, but teacher thinks everything is "sooooo good!" Thereby, the teacher actually teaches students nondiscrimination. You might well remember something you considered really good that you accomplished as a child and a teacher disapproved, but did you ever do something you thought was really bad and yet have an adult say "I like it very much?"

One might say that creativity is an expression from the inside which has not been inhibited by societal wants and needs. Once inhibited it is difficult to regain. How are you going to go about teaching creativity? Will the water colors dry up and crack before your students find out what they are for or will all of your students paint red houses with blue skies? Is it possible to instruct too much or to judge students too early in life? Have you known of students in elementary school who were told not to sing because of poor pitch or a raucous tone quality? How can a teacher keep the creative doors open? Do teachers who shut doors for children intend to judge them that harshly? Are children more creative when they are young and progressively get less and less so as they grow older? Or are they taught to be less creative? How might learning "rules of harmony" be approached while encouraging creativity? *How much instruction, when,* and *who should evaluate what* are important issues regarding creativity.

Another final aspect for teachers concerns how much creativity they actually will tolerate. That is, do teachers believe in creativity only for those things that do matter too much? "You may be as creative as you can when you finger paint so long as you stay on the paper." "You may *not* read creatively." "Of course you may calculate creatively if you get the right answer." Very often novel responses are not tolerated if they interfere with established rules or customs. If you as a prospective teacher believe that creativity ought to be a *vital* part of the curriculum, then how might you go about it? How much creation? In what areas?

Allowing for creativity usually means that teachers decide certain innocuous activities are appropriate for their students to be creative in. It seems many teachers cannot, unfortunately, handle much creativity in any direction. Many teachers are unwilling to permit much verbal disagreement on creative spelling or reading without the rationalization that everybody has different techniques, as long as they all get the same answer.

It is often the case that certain school activities may be deemed as being incompatible with creativity. If a student develops a personal method of spelling words, then the student defeats the purpose of learning to spell; namely, to enable effective communication of ideas in written form to others. It is maintained that if a child's spelling is not the same as the accepted system then no one but the child will be able to read what has been written. And what does the student learn from the process? To spell certainly. But is that all?

Process versus product, tangible reorganization of past experience versus that which is mystical and unexplainable, instruction versus no instruction, evaluation versus no evaluation, freedom to explore versus freedom to explore only that which is good. . . .

Wut is kreativit?

4

WHEN SHALL WE TEACH?

WHEN IS TODAY?

When has to do with time. Life is a series of activities in time, yet our greatest difficulty in life seems to center around our inability to tell time. For example, consider the phrase "the end justifies the means." What does it mean when people say the end justifies the means? Do they mean that the result obtained is worth whatever one has to go through to get it? A college degree is fine but not all that work; a diet is fine because you will look and feel better; war is justifiable because at its end there will be a much better world—or alternately, war is justifiable because when the end comes things would be worse without the means. Usually "the means" in the preceding phrases refers to something derogatory. Also, in many cases, even the *end* is unsure. Another example of this inability to tell time is exemplified when the prospective teacher states, "I want to be a good teacher (end); therefore, I go through these bad courses (means)."

Historically, many have argued we would have a better world if only we could get through the bad means. Hitler sought annihilation of several million people (means) to realize his dream of an Aryan "super race" (end). In the process a lot of people would be liquidated (derogatory means), but the resulting world (end) would justify the means.

Alternately, it has been said that when the end is uncertain it is wrong to justify terrible means to accomplish it. Bertrand Russell abhorred war as too monstrous a means for any end. He would have said that having a war in order to bring about a better world is ridiculous because war is the worst possible thing imaginable. Therefore, when the end (of war) comes, what does it bring? Some would say that at best it brings the absence of war.

Should one justify terrible means for an unsure end? If as students you endure academic misery, will you as teachers be able to achieve academic happiness? What does it mean to become a teacher? Does it mean that we are certified? Qualified? Or does it mean that we have established so much love for living and learning we want to share it with others? What transpires between here and there that makes us actual teachers? To ask the question another way, *When do we take responsibility for our lives?* Today? Tomorrow? When we get out of this class? After we graduate? When after that? When we become teachers? Principals? When are we students? When *are* we teachers?

If there is a causal connection between a specified means and a desired end then we might assume a cause-and-effect world—that is, assuming a time line from cause to effect. We might engage in the process of *becoming,* where each end is a beginning. What are the indications along the time line that the means are affecting the end? Will the world really be a better place after some people are eliminated, after a new president is elected, or when we have become teachers? Do negative means produce positive ends? Are happy students happy teachers? Are unhappy students happy teachers? If students go through misery do they become miserable? What makes the difference? How do we justify what happens from one point to another on the time line? What negatives along the line at some point turn into positives, into happiness? On a time line, where is the end? Where are the means?

Some people associate means and ends with power. An old joke states: Just give me some power, then we will have a better world; I'm not responsible because I do not have any power to do anything about the situation. Give me power and "comes the revolution we have strawberries and cream." What? "Comes the revolution we have strawberries and cream." But I don't like strawberries and cream. "Comes the revolution we have strawberries and cream OR YOU DIE!"

Some associate means and ends with organizational ability. For example, a person is working in a tar pit digging tar with several other people. He says, "If you elect me supervisor of the tar diggers I'll organize you and we'll dig more tar." And then he gets to be supervisor of the tar diggers and he says, "You know, I'd really like to help you dig more tar but my boss, the guy who is the supervisor of the tar pit supervisors, bothers me. Now, if I had his job, I could affect the needed changes in the tar pit." As supervisor of supervisors he says, "I really want to get that tar dug, that *is* what I want to do." Then he wants to be the supervisor of the supervisors of the supervisors, and so on, because there is always somebody over him who has power such that he "cannot do his job." Finally he becomes President of Tar, but now he cannot dig tar because "I am too far removed from the pit" and besides "the corporate board makes certain demands." "If only I were Chairman of the Board. . . ."

In education there are supervisors, and supervisors of supervisors (some have different names)—yet, there is always room for the rationalization: "The end is such that if you let me get to the point where I have power, then I can really change things; otherwise, do not give me the responsibility because I'm just following orders. Besides, it has always been done this way." Make the above analogy more real by substituting your own situation. For example, the authors state "I really love kids. I'm really concerned about kids. I love kids so much that I'm not teaching kids. I'm going to teach teachers of kids! Next year I get to teach teachers of teachers of kids." Try the above on yourself. What tar do you want dug? If one has to give away too much (rationalize) to get the power, then does one have sufficient power such that one can actually change the system? People who make a case for means versus ends cannot tell time. If one defines a point in time, then should one be certain concerning what is end and what is means? Is one particular thing the means to only one end? Or is that end the means to some other end? When, in time, does the end become the end? Maybe when we are eating strawberries and cream!

When does one prepare to become a teacher? After one graduates? School work represents a lot of misery until one engages in school work (teaches). When do you prepare to become a good teacher? It has been suggested that a good student will continue those behaviors after graduation. Does it bother you to think that bad or mediocre students (means) might become bad or mediocre teachers (ends)? "But A students are not always the best teachers." Or are they? What are you doing right now (means) concerning your personal development in your lessons, with your roommate, with your parents, with people you contact, and especially with youngsters you contact? Consider this monolog: "I don't spend time with children right here on campus but when I become a teacher I am going to really know my students." "I do not read the newspapers and I do not really know what is going on in the world because I am so busy —you just don't realize how much time I spend in the library. However, when I get to be a teacher I'm going to help my students be aware of the world around them. (Don't they still have those *Weekly Readers*?)"

When do you become a teacher? When does the transformation begin? When do you become informed and involved? When do you become alive? When are you concerned? What are you doing now to become what you want to be? What are you doing to become that kind of person you want children to emulate? Are you now going through some magic behaviors such that at some point you turn into something else? Is there a disparity between your means and ends, between your ideas and behaviors? One is reminded of the rich man who constantly eats potato soup. When asked why he eats potato soup all the time he replies "So I can save my money and will not ever have to eat potato soup!" If your means are not identical with your ends, then perhaps you have something confused. Did you skip class as part of your preparation for becoming a great teacher?

It could be that only *means* are "real" in the progression of life's activities and that today is always the first day of the rest of your life.

When is today?

WHEN IS TOO SOON?

One of the most problematic aspects of teaching concerns developmental processes. The question is *when* to teach *what* to the child. In our attempt to communicate with the child we often create much confusion and even misinformation that must be corrected at some time in the future. A child asks a question and we try to explain to the child; then we end by saying, "Well, that is not really the way it is, but for right now it is all right." We know that we have not given the child a complete or even perhaps a true answer, but we just do not know how to explain at a level the child can understand.

A good negative example of this problem concerns the time signature in music notation. Many texts present the child with the explanation that the bottom number in ($\frac{3}{4}$) represents the beat note and the top number represents the number of beat notes per measure. For numerous signatures this is misinformation and will not adequately explain such common musical examples as the signature $\frac{3}{4}$ in the "Star Spangled Banner" (in which the quarter note is indeed the beat note) and the $\frac{3}{4}$ in the "Blue Danube Waltz" (in which the dotted half, not the quarter note, serves as the beat). It might be conjectured that not only does the above "standard definition" concerning time signatures not represent the actual case but represents inert subject matter not important for the elementary or secondary student—or perhaps not even important to advanced musicians. Regardless, teachers often try to explain to the young child and in so doing create misinformation because of the oversimplicity of the explanation. Thus, students are continuously unlearning and relearning because teachers cannot find ways to give them "truth" that does not require constant modification. It should be pointed out that inability to explain extant knowledge differs from inability to explain new knowledge and should not be confused with advancements concerning *new* discoveries throughout time. Knowledge is in constant ferment and new information must be incorporated into any teaching technique even though there may be some confusion in the process. There does seem to be much extant knowledge that can be taught without the confusion that presently exists for the developing child.

Some may think that the preceding paragraph overstates the argument and that simplifying information so children can understand is indeed beneficial. What students are told does not have to be a misconception. Yet, if a child asks a question that has a difficult and involved answer and we give the child that complete answer, the child may very well feel frustrated because he misunderstands or knows no more than before. However, if this knowledge is simplified so that the student can comprehend it, the student will probably be much happier, even though it is not the *entire* explanation. Learning is a growing-up process and as a child grows, understanding will increase to the point where the child can comprehend more. *Too soon* may be when the child is not ready physically or mentally and becomes frustrated by this inability to comprehend.

What aspects of child development are relevant, even crucial, in teaching the child music? Jerome Bruner begins Chapter Three of *The Process of Education* with the hypothesis that "any subject matter can be taught effectively in some intellectually honest form to any child at any stage of development." He suggests that there is never a point in time during a child's life that is too soon to begin instruction. This appears an admirable goal, and while difficult, may represent the best possible way of not having to reteach because of initial simple explanations (that is, $\frac{3}{4}$ indicates the quarter gets the beat) that must subsequently be changed because they do not represent complete information.

Additionally, other qualified and respected authorities (for example, Piaget) are concerned with other aspects of developmental stages and the necessity of realizing certain limitations concerning levels of development. Obviously, all aspects of the child's developmental growth should be considered carefully in structuring music experiences. However, a final point should be made concerning combining all the respected positions into a compatible whole. While many theories of education are complementary, certain issues should be thought through carefully. For example, in contrast to Bruner's statement, Piaget asserts that abstract thought is not possible before 10 or 11 years of age. It would seem that if we are to accept the seemingly disparate aspects of these men's work we must first think through clearly those aspects of their theories that appear compatible as well as those that are not. Perhaps there are aspects of subject matter that prepare the child at an early age for more "formal operations" later on. Perhaps apparent conflict can be rationalized or explained. However, it does not appear that productive thinking is enhanced when educators maintain that everybody has some "good ideas" about how children learn without going into some detail concerning these good ideas. If a child cannot abstractly think before age 10, then a teacher might endeavor to provide the child with experiences that prepare for abstract thinking later on. Obviously, many other things can be taught that do not require abstract thought. Yet, the conflict is not resolved. Some educators have never had to go into detail about seeming conflict because they mistakenly espouse what they consider an "eclectic philosophy" which gives credence to taking little bits of this and that, mixing it up, and coming out with a compatible whole. However, this "whole" may or may not represent the actual case. All aspects regarding the child's growth need to be thought through very carefully by the teacher, and must then be combined with extremely careful observation of each child.

Even though many educators advocate an eclectic position, many viewpoints as espoused by various authorities or methodological positions may not be compatible. This is because they exclude each other and, therefore, putting them together would be illogical. Some music teachers say that it is never too soon to teach aspects of any music phenomenon, and others maintain that there are precise developmental stages through which children must go to be able to succeed at certain kinds of aesthetic, intellectual, and performing activities. The above example is just one of many. Important decisions must be made concerning such issues as: Is there such a thing as reading readiness in music? At what age should students enter a band program? A string program? Chorus? Can complex rhythms be learned by students at all ages? What is indeed too abstract? When do students value music? In what ways do children move to music? When? How does development theory help structure our music program?

When is too soon?

WHEN IS PROGRESS?

How do teachers know when students improve? The assessment of improvement is much easier in academic than in social behaviors of students. A teacher notes progress when a student can solve a new problem, sing better in tune, or answer questions orally. In short, academic behaviors are easily assessed or measured because these behaviors can be observed and counted. Indeed, most people expect concrete evidence of academic behavior. Teachers do not say about a standardized test, "I saw Billy taking that test today and I can just feel that his score is 83." One never assesses academic behavior without actually observing it in some manner. Therefore, the *idea* of academic improvement by itself rarely satisfies a teacher. It is much like the bank keeping tabs on one's checking account. When one gets a notice of overdraft one does not call the bank officer to say that he *feels* pretty good about his checking account, therefore, it must be all right. Obviously, there is a certain amount of bookkeeping necessary to keep an accurate assessment of what one's balance (or academic achievement) actually is.

In reference to the above, the question might be asked: Is teaching the same thing as learning? Because a concept has been taught, does that mean that it has been learned? A teacher teaches Billy the material covered on a test. Does the teacher still need to give him the test? Is teaching enough? Can we measure the teaching? Can we measure the learning? In our present age of accountability most of the answers have been provided for us. Academic behavior covering both teacher and learner must be documented and periodically assessed.

What if the behaviors one is interested in teaching are not academic subject matters but social behaviors or values: "I want my students to be kind, honest, take pride in our group, and accepting of all their classmates." Kindness is an idea. How can a teacher get a student to learn the idea of kindness? Should the student just be told many times to be kind? Is that enough? What about specific examples for the student to emulate? Should the teacher point out examples of kindness as they occur day by day? Should the teacher have one "honesty" lesson and then go on to something else? How can the teacher get at least one student to engage in a behavior that falls into the category of honesty so that the teacher can use the student as an example? Can one measure the instances of kindness and honesty that occur in a classroom? Perhaps the teacher can count how many instances occur in a specific time period (the number per day, per week, per hour). If the instances increase, then they are getting better; however, if the instances in the specific time period decrease, then they are getting worse. Progress concerning even intangibles relating to a student's character sometimes can be measured and demonstrated.

Some teachers state that progress ought to be represented and measured here and now, that is, when the student is still a student of a particular teacher. They maintain that long-term effects seem more probable when a little progress is evident *now*. Other teachers, especially in the arts, state repeatedly that they are developing *future* taste and appreciation. It may be that appreciation is like a late-blooming flower. On the other hand it may be continuous and progressive. Is taste a matter of constant development and assessment? Perhaps it only becomes evident when the student is in next year's class. Taste may be late blooming and yet skill development continuous. Teachers engaged in instrumental music usually assess skill development continuously. Perhaps long-term cognitive and affective behavior should also receive continuous attention.

Progress is difficult to assess without the standard measuring instruments that account for the child's development and growth. While many tools exist to assess cognitive skills, the affective domain still appears to be more inferential and illusive. Recently more and more scholars have been working in areas of the affective domain.* Perhaps tools will be developed whereby the teacher can make assessments concerning the child's inner world, perhaps even to the point at which the student begins to self-evaluate. Hopefully, teachers will be continuously concerned with "When Is Progress?" as a tangible fact and not as a rationalization to eschew the responsibility of making temporal judgments. Assessment should always be used to determine where the student should go from here and should not be used as a static evaluation.

Progress in the academic world is said to have taken place when someone understands, comprehends, or has a better mastery of a subject. Such progress is often measured with a test. Yet some students get nervous and anxious in taking a test, and, though they maintain that they thought they knew the material, they do poorly and are then evaluated as having made little or no progress. Others appear to do better on exams, especially objective ones, with less knowledge of the subject. This suggests that our assessment instruments are often fallible and incomplete indicators of progress. Assessment of learning must be carefully structured. If such is not the case, parents may assume that their child progressed when a report card grade rose from D to C when, in reality, the child may not have learned much or even progressed. He just got a C.

When is Progress?

*See Part III.

WHEN IS INDEPENDENCE?

Two worthwhile goals of teachers are (1) making themselves dispensable as soon as possible (teaching for student independence), and (2) teaching students to believe and select only that which makes sense. Both goals aim at teaching independence.

The first goal—making teachers dispensable as soon as possible— seems somewhat contradictory to current teaching practice. The model for most music student-teacher interactions is one of strong authority. Yet it seems difficult for a teacher to respect the individual dignity of each student and allow for individual differences when the teacher presumes a complete authoritative role. Many students come to depend on the teacher in lieu of parental guidance and independent thinking (some teachers even take on the role of psychologist or physician). In such a case, teaching is no longer a question of "showing the way" but becomes a situation of "telling what to do." Unfortunately, some teachers want nothing more than to tell students what to do. A partial answer to this question concerns *when* should the student achieve independence. In the earliest stages strong guidance may be advisable, even preferred; but *when* will students learn to develop their own taste and establish their own values?

Considering the development of the child and the child's inability to learn from nothing (that is, to learn in the absence of stimuli) it seems that the teacher must maintain some aspects of the child's environment just to get the youngster started. The paramount issue then for the teacher is not *if* independence, but *when*. If one is concerned about the student's independence then the child should be given more and more opportunities to select learning materials and experiences. The ideal situation would be to have the student's achievement of absolute independence coincide with the termination of the formal learning experience. This is probably impossible, yet the teacher should begin early to encourage the student's own selection of music; development of individual verbalizations concerning taste, and productive use of leisure time. This technique represents a procedure which gives increasing responsibility to the learner. Many teachers say that they believe in student independence but do not set up specific experiences in which students can begin to take responsibility for learning.

The second goal, teaching students to believe only that which makes sense to them, is sometimes difficult to achieve. It is especially difficult when students try and try again yet fail until they create a "need" to find an answer that has been immediately apparent to the teacher. At such times teachers feel that time is wasted waiting for students to "discover" needs, wants, and desires—or even correct answers. However, one should keep in mind that both teacher and student could be wrong or right. If a teacher is wrong, only the most independent student will argue or contradict. If the teacher is strong, then the teacher may also be removing any source of constructive feedback for the teacher.

A major goal for the student is to develop a life style over time that includes some ability to analyze, criticize, and choose alternatives consistent with some value hierarchy. This final result may be achieved when students help select music, decide on creative evaluation, correct a test, develop and evaluate a test, develop a music appreciation calendar, develop the concert program, help others within the ensemble decide how good some music is, decide how good they are as performing musicians and as creating musicians or as consumer musicians, when they can select future music experiences on the basis of detailed knowledge, when they have developed enough skill to at least appreciate the musical skill evidenced in others, when they realize that musical taste may be made up of other components than just liking, when they can create their own musical environment. In other words, ideally students should be able to choose for themselves when they are aware of many musical alternatives and understand the issues relating to the "good" as well as the "real" choices within their life's experiences.

When is independence?

5

HOW SHALL WE TEACH?

HOW SHOULD TEACHERS BEHAVE?

Each one of us has quite definite ideas about how we want to behave and ought to behave. Yet for some, ideas and behaviors never quite get together. ("I'm always eating potato soup so I can save my money and never have to eat potato soup.") It is generally useful for prospective teachers to try putting ideas of what they want their life styles to be into practice; that is, to try projecting their ideal life styles into specific day-to-day behaviors. For instance, "I want to be nice to children" is an idea. How might such an idea be actualized? What specific children and what specific behaviors follow from the idea? How much time will be required to implement that idea?

Once one decides what it is that one is about (actually this amounts to deciding just who you are) cannot one then begin to act on this knowledge as expediently, efficiently, and happily as possible? Many people create a disparity between the way they *say* they choose to live and how they actually *do* live. There exists a difference between ideas and behaviors, between what people think and what they do. "I love children very much, but I just can't find enough time to spend with them, especially here at school."

What if one finds that one's behaviors do not coincide with the kind of life one chooses? What can be done about it? Some say one should begin by *acting* one's way into a new way of *thinking* because this is easier than *thinking* your way into a new way of *acting*.

In the preceding pages we discussed *values*. This chapter concerns techniques for implementing whatever values teachers choose to teach their students. These particular behavior techniques represent the authors' biases and should be so regarded. It is the authors' belief that if a teacher values quietness in the classroom, then behavioral techniques can help bring quietness about. Another teacher may value a higher noise level, another may choose to have the children decide (by action or default). Behavioral techniques can be used to bring almost any situation into existence. However, one should not mistake the *techniques* used to implement teacher values for the *values themselves*. This situation of separating as well as combining values and techniques may be viewed as a *static-temporal, means-ends problem.* *

An effective structure for teaching specific behaviors includes the following four steps: (1) pinpoint, (2) record, (3) consequate, and (4) evaluate. One first pinpoints those specific behaviors which, according to the teacher's value system, should either increase or decrease. The number of those behaviors presently occurring is recorded. Then the teacher consequates by setting up the teaching strategy, positively reinforcing subsequent appropriate student behaviors, and disapproving inappropriate student behaviors. Evaluation consists of recording once again to determine whether the behaviors are increasing or decreasing. The following example clarifies this structure of teaching:

Pinpoint: Students in chorus are not watching the teacher while performing.

*See Part III.

Record: Seventy-eight instances of students looking away from teacher are observed during a fifteen-minute performance.

Consequate: Specific students who *were* watching were praised after the performance. Students observed watching the teacher during rehearsals were given verbal praise and told how important eye contact was.

Evaluate: Instances of students not watching the teacher decreased to eight during a fifteen-minute period.

The question is sometimes asked, "How do students learn to respond to the teacher's praise?" Do the people you know, at college or in your own family, respond to your praise? Many students have *not* learned to respond to the teacher's praise, verbal or physical, or even to respond to activities. Perhaps some children have not received much praise from parents. In this case the teacher must decide: "Should I structure in order to teach students to respond to my style or will I use techniques that their parents use?"

How do students begin to like the things they learn to like? Can they still learn to like a subject when the teacher is threatening, disapproving, and insensitive to student ideas, work, and feelings? Will you make your expectancies known to your students, both for academic work and social behavior? Some teachers call such expectancies *class rules.* How will your students find out that your expectancies are different in different types of activities? You might structure for that. Class rules are statements of contingent classroom relationships: "If you talk quietly during this activity, get your instrument out quietly, and watch me when we sing, then I will be pleased with you." You should also remember that class rules may change from one activity to another.

Disagreement concerning what educational methodology is best or appropriate in certain situations could result from the different ways in which the world is viewed (different values) or from the particular strengths and weaknesses of individual teachers. There is tremendous variety concerning methodological procedure. Each prospective teacher should begin early to decide which method or methods to use.

As in the means-ends discussion, it is suggested that one *do* the kinds of things that one thinks about. Can one be a generous person without performing acts of generosity? Does an honest person deal in dishonesties? Can one be a good student and neglect to study and learn? It may be wise to consider the process whereby prospective teachers begin to *act* as they plan to act when they become teachers. Consider the college student who complains daily about school work during the four years of college: "I can't go. I *have* to study. I'll be glad to get this awful paper finished. Oh, that's a boring class." This same student may believe that complaining comes "naturally." Perhaps it would be better for this student to begin finding things that are good in education and developing positive verbal responses for a few months.

Hopefully, one chooses how to live life and then sets about doing things and behaving in such a way that no disparity exists between the idea of how life is lived and the actual behavior. If there is a disparity it might be called a life-style gap, a personal credibility gap, or perhaps even an integrity quotient.

How should teachers behave?

HOW DO TEACHERS CHOOSE TO ACT?

"You cannot fool animals and small children." This old cliché implies that a child can detect phoniness and always spot a fake. Teachers are often admonished to "be yourself, be natural." But what if the natural "us" is not what we would like to be—what if there is a disparity between our ideas and behaviors?

Do teachers sometimes live such disparities of which they may be unaware—perhaps because they are afraid—afraid of losing a job, afraid of students, afraid of facing themselves, or afraid of making a real choice? Outside pressure often determines the way people choose to act. However, if a teacher wants students to learn to choose independently, then should not the teacher be the first to act in accordance with this belief? Will a teacher's students learn independence based upon knowledge of alternatives if the teacher allows outside pressures to structure activities rather than consistent choice based upon the teacher's own value hierarchy?

What if a teacher or prospective teacher is very negative? This could have been learned through years of negative interactions and four college years of complaining; the product of such learning being one who has become negative in behavior, if not in desire. What if the *end* (goal) is to be a positive teacher in the classroom, yet the day-to-day *means* (behavior) is distant, cold, or even bitter? Should a teacher then *act?* Should a teacher ever pretend? Should a teacher behave in a manner uncomfortable for the teacher? Should a teacher "act" positive instead of being "naturally" negative?

A great deal of evidence suggests that teachers want to be more approving than disapproving in the classroom. Teachers verbalize that they would rather say nice things and compliment their students as opposed to telling them what is wrong and being critical most of the time. However, when these same teachers are observed in their classrooms a very small percentage actually gives more approval than disapproval to their students.* Consider once again the disparity between what people say and what they do. Very few teachers actually achieve their own value system. Should these same teachers continue to be disapproving because it feels "natural" to them? Or should they "act their way into a new way of thinking" because they would then be doing what they said (and perhaps actually believe) they want to be doing?

Other considerations follow from teachers acting "naturally." Suppose a first grader comes into class crying. Should one wait until he stops crying to pick him up? Or should he be picked up to stop his

*See bibliography.

crying? Probably the teacher's natural reaction would be to pick him up immediately. Yet if behavior is a result of its consequences it would be better to wait for a period of time after he stopped crying. If he is picked up during or immediately after the crying then crying behavior is reinforced (rewarded). Teachers who make this mistake either do not fully understand the contingencies of behavior or cannot tell time (remember the means-ends time discussion). One could stop the child's crying very quickly (this time) by picking him up; but, in rewarding his crying one may actually be teaching him to cry again the next time he wants attention.* Issues concerning cause and effect relationships are not very complicated to understand but the behaviors involved are tremendously hard to elicit. In the beginning stages evoking certain behavior is not natural and takes practice. In the above case you have to wait long enough for the child to equate your attention with his proper behavior. What if you think the child has been hurt? An easy first test is to pick him up and see if he stops crying immediately. If he does, then you know that he was not hurt. He was crying for your attention—and now that you picked him up he will cry a little longer next time. Yet if you are consistent in the future he will respond without crying.

How can a teacher get students to behave as the teacher wants or within the boundaries of creativity the teacher has established? Most teachers constantly criticize and tell the student what is wrong because such behavior "comes naturally" to the teacher. If a teacher really wants to be approving how is this to be achieved if current teacher–student interactions are of a disapproving nature? What does one do? Obviously, one begins to engage in behaviors that will make one a little more positive. One practices and does more than merely think about interaction patterns (ideas).

One might say, "But what if Jim just cannot sing? How can I approve of him then?" In this case the teacher might say, "Jim, I really like the way you are trying and participating." Jim can thus be reinforced for appropriate social behavior. If academic feedback is also neces-

*See Part III.

sary the teacher might say, "Jim, you are singing too loudly and off-key" and then later compliment Jim for listening to instructions, or for some other desirable social behavior.

Reinforcers, compliments, or feedback, to be effective, must follow student behaviors. In dealing with strictly academic subjects this feedback generally consists of correcting answers. No one would expect students to go long periods of time without academic feedback. But what about social behaviors? Are students ever complimented for how well they behave? Or do teachers typically wait until students misbehave and then attend to them ("Stop that!")? The norm usually consists of situations similar to the crying of the first grader. Teachers need to get negative/positive interaction patterns turned around. Perhaps teachers might indicate their delight when students behave appropriately—whether the teacher "feels" comfortable about it or not. "But you can't fool those kids." Perhaps, but in time you can "fool" yourself into becoming real and sincere—*if* the original idea is sincere.

Sincerity poses another question at this point. Is not an interaction less real, less sincere if the teacher must structure, plan, and practice to be positive? Would it not be better to let the student know how you really feel? Yes. Sometimes. . . . Perhaps the real question ought to be: Is *lack* of structure inherently better than capricious occurrence? If persons work at a relationship, does that make the interaction dishonest? Suppose one really wishes to do something nice for a friend or loved one and writes it on a calendar and really plans it. The friend then receives a nice gift on that special day but finds that it was planned. Does that make it wrong, less desirable than a capricious, impulsive action? What if your boyfriend (or girlfriend) came to a counselor and said that he was not really as nice to you as he chose to be and the counselor asked him what nice things he could think of doing. The counselor might tell him to make sure that he actually does those things and keeps a record of the things he really does, if he wants to change. So, he comes up to you and does one of those really nice things, takes out his pencil, marks it down and you ask, "What are you doing?" He replies, "I'm working at improving our relationship." Would your response be, "*Well,* don't do me any favors! "?

Behavioral patterns are often even more subtle. Suppose a teacher was brought up in an environment of racial prejudice. Sometimes prejudice can be very subtle. Perhaps as a very young child while walking with father, the child felt the father's hand tighten every time they passed a person of another race. Even though father always said that no one should be prejudiced and believed everyone deserved love and acceptance, the little child remembered that tightening of the hand . . . and could never quite understand the feeling of being uncomfortable around those "lovely" people or realize why he had a difficult time accepting them. Later, as a teacher, this same person may find it intellectually compatible but physically difficult to touch those "lovely children." Should an effort then be made to act one's way into a new way of thinking—to touch, to interact, and to accept? Even if it is at first difficult and unnatural? How does the whole aspect of body language affect teacher–student interactions?

Does the effect of the behavior lessen if one thinks about it, and therefore plans and structures? Some would believe that spontaneity is the only aspect of a personal relationship in or out of education that really matters; that is, if anything is planned the effect is somehow lessened. "Don't be nice to me, if you just really want to be nice to me then you can, but if you have to plan for it, then NO." Should an ingrained habit be given more credence than thoughtful change?

It is good to be sincere, acting and reacting to students spontaneously when one feels good and is enjoying teaching. However, should one bring bad moods to school and behave surly toward students because that is the way one feels that day? Is it not necessary at times to hide one's true feelings—especially when dealing with impressionable children? If a teacher is sincere about wanting to be a good teacher, then acting pleasant when really feeling bad or being patient with a student who "should know better" may not necessarily be "phoney." It may represent only a temporary adjustment in order to be *consistent* in attaining one's final goal. If one chooses being positive as a value choice, then the *negative* behavior would then be insincere or hypocritical.

How do teachers choose to act?

HOW IMPORTANT IS STRUCTURE?

Behavioral techniques applied to the implementation of a value system differ from the means-ends dichotomy in that the techniques begin to implement values *immediately.* For instance, the idea of "kindness" as an end may be nebulous and non-behavioral. If, however, kind acts are defined such that people agree upon what constitutes acting kindly, then a behavioral technique consists of getting students to do such acts and then reinforcing the kind behavior with positive activities, things, or personal interactions. Thus, means (techniques) and ends (values) become identical in temporal, real-life situations. In such a situation our money saver in the preceding pages at any certain time would (1) eat potato soup because he likes and wants to eat potato soup, (2) not eat potato soup because he does not want to eat it, or (3) defines at precisely what point he has eaten enough potato soup in order to have saved enough money.

Another important concept related to structure and the means-ends, values-techniques comparisons concerns the idea of *readiness* and where to begin in the teaching-learning process. If learning is defined as the elicitation of what one already knows in association with new contexts (the reorganization of past experiences) then the teacher has no problem *if* students have already learned. What if our students have not already learned? How does one draw from an empty well? Do children learn to sing by imitation or do they just "begin" when they are ready without any help? Most people believe that in order for children to learn they need a model to imitate. If some children do not need a model and already sing, then the teacher has no problem. The readiness concept can present a problem if teachers use it as an excuse not to teach. For instance, consider this dialogue: "Why isn't Johnny learning to read?" "Because, he is not ready." "When will he be ready?" "It is difficult to say, but we will know when he is ready." "How?" "Well, he will begin to read. . . . " So far Johnny is in first and second grades; however, by third grade if Johnny cannot read it is because of his "bad" first and second grade teachers. Eventually, every student gets to a point where lack of "readiness" will not explain lack of achievement. At that point someone must take reponsibility to *define those experiences* which lead to readiness. If the child has no skills in music listening, aural discrimination, symbolic imagery, right-left orientation, and so on, then the child must be taught the skills necessary to integrate these facets of music in order to *read* music. There is a difference between defining and providing necessary experiences and waiting for "readiness."

If we wait for someone to love us before we love them, we may wait forever. Likewise, if we wait until the child demonstrates readiness, independently, we may wait a long, long time. Instead we could carefully set up those environmental sequences which will bring the child into contact with materials and ideas and cause the child to *want* to begin learning. Some prospective teachers say they do not believe in *any* structure. But, of course, they have not really thought it through. The degree or kind of structure should not be confused with the act of structuring. The person who really does not believe in structuring would not become a teacher. Structure begins when two people meet or even when one becomes aware of one's environment. Some teachers take great care in structuring the physical environment; others structure the interpersonal environment; while others structure the academic environment. Regardless, from analysis of our physical environment through analysis of Mozart, to being aware one exists, organization is evident. The investigation and manipulation of this environment then becomes paramount.

How important is structure?

HOW MUCH GOOD CAN WE DO?

Let us summarize the important issues that have been previously presented. Assuming that you, the prospective teacher, are going to accept at least some responsibility for helping your students learn, one can ask the question, "How much good can be done?" "How much difference can we make?" Keeping in mind all of the influences that impinge upon any student—parents, peers, neighbors, and the community—what values can we expect to prevail in the child's life? How much will our role matter? Can we open new avenues for students? Can we offer the students new choices that previously did not exist by providing direct experiences as well as vicarious learning situations? Can we be sure that the student actually *does* something as opposed to just thinking or talking about it?

Consider this statement: "I don't like all that structure and those behavioral techniques. I don't want my children to sit up straight in their chairs all the time. I want a creative classroom." What is wrong? The statement implies that the goals and the techniques are identical and that only one goal can be taught behaviorally. It ignores the fact that behavioral techniques can be used to bring about any goals desired: pandemonium, creativity, loudness, softness, or chairsitting. The techniques themselves are based on the very simple premise that behavior is the result of its consequences. Who *decides* what kind of feedback or consequences to give to students? You will, academically and socially. *Will students want to help decide?* Hopefully, especially if you teach them to decide. Can you reinforce them for decision making? Yes.

Let us consider a relatively unimportant issue to use as an example: How would you ensure that a person had a choice among 50 ice cream flavors? How would you go about teaching your students or children to have a choice among 50 flavors? In the first place you must have a *subject matter* and in this case it is ice cream. The ability to make a decision constitutes the goal or the end (value). You would also need the accoutrements of the subject matter: scoops, cones, ice cream flavors, and so on. Then you might have them taste all the flavors (that is, direct as opposed to vicarious sampling of the ice cream). Vicarious learning is learning from somebody else's behavior or something you can project from your own. There are some things that can be taught vicariously and there are some things that students must learn directly. In the case of ice cream, must each individual child taste for himself? How much direct experience and how much vicarious learning should be provided? Can a student have a feeling for the consequences regarding certain acts (violence, murder) without actually doing them? Can one appreciate the Sistine Chapel of Michelangelo without lying on one's back for several years? Is one not able to learn from *vicarious* as well as from *direct* experience?

There is also the issue of *censorship* and *selectivity:* the problem with sampling all 50 ice cream flavors directly is that it requires a great deal of *time.* There is a lot of subject matter and it obviously cannot all be covered. ("I do not want to indoctrinate my musical values: I want my students to establish their own values in music.") Yet students are only going to have the flavors of ice cream that they know. And if they never experience butter-nut-fudge directly (if they never hear that kind of music) then they do not have that experience from which to choose. "I want children to choose their own value system for themselves." Yet, what are the *real* choices? Children only choose from what they already know. These issues must be decided by you, the prospective teacher, and they have little to do with your teaching techniques: they have to do with values.

Teaching might then begin with students sampling all 50 flavors (or 50 different aspects of music)—unless there is a point to be made for vicarious learning about the ice cream (music) curriculum, or unless you choose to teach something besides selection. You might do it day by day having students sample five flavors a day. However, you should beware of satiation or saturation. And how much should you expose then to at a certain time? The issue again concerns selectivity and censorship. Before one gets to specific techniques implementing choice, it might be that the first thing we would want to do is have students taste all the different flavors (or experience all types of music). After students taste them all, you might have them choose. Yet what if they "choose" the same one again and again? In this instance the teacher may say: "You may pick any flavor except the one you selected last time." This procedure places a restriction on choice in order to assure broader experience.

If your student has tasted chocolate, strawberry, and vanilla five times each and you then say "choose the one you like best," then the student may have some direct experience upon which to act. But if you have students choose any flavor on any basis, and at the same time *tell* them they are "choosing," you may create other problems. The student is no longer choosing from direct experience but is acting capriciously. The above argument is not intended to make a point for one method against another; it is intended to point out the difference. A prospective teacher should discriminate between being asked to choose in the presence of facts, reason, and past history and choosing capriciously. A choice concerning any aspect of subject matter can be real or it can be capricious. Besides teaching choice relating to different music one might also consider teaching about color, texture, form, design, or anything else that might make an impression on the students.

What if you wanted to ensure: (1) that the student actually believes a choice exists, and (2) that the student chooses strawberry (classical music) only. What might you do? As a technique you might prepare a very bad tasting ice cream, give him an excellent testing strawberry, and then let him decide. That is much like the verbal statements: "Do you want to go to a good sensible school or that awful Podunk U.?" "Do you want to go to college or do you want to be a failure?" "Are you going to just learn or are you going to major in something practical?" "Do you like to listen to *that* junk?" Some people who go to college think they have had a choice, while actually the choice has been *good* but not *real*.

Another technique is to *tell* students that they have a choice. Not *give* them direct experience, just tell them. In reading some books one often finds a statement such as "this is not the *only* way" after which the author goes on and on describing only one way. Only one point of view is presented but somehow the reader believes there was a choice involved because the author said so. Why does the reader think the author is broadminded and considers other points of view? Because the author says it a lot! "I have a choice (because somebody told me I do)" represents the most frightening kind of indoctrination. "I've never been any place but the United States and it's the best country in the world. I just know it is." In contrast to what? "To all those places I know are bad." How do you know those places are so bad? "I just know they are." As a prospective teacher if you want to teach choice such that people believe that they have it, yet actually do not, *tell* them they have a choice. Tell them many times.

Consider the American who declared to the French chef that he has never tasted anything but American food—and that it is the best in the world. What about the ice cream: do you think the teacher ought to use direct *or* vicarious experiences? Do students really need to taste all those flavors? Or can they get what they need vicariously? Vicarious learning seems appropriate in regard to negative or harmful situations, to small or innocuous aspects of the curriculum (ice cream), or in freeing time to be spent on more meaningful learnings.

Additionally, it would seem that there are many things that need to be taught vicariously just because there is not enough time to teach everything—even if the teacher knows everything. How many musics, histories, religions, flavors do you need to know to be a good teacher? In the field of subject matter what is available, and how should it be taught? Does one just take the music that comes from the existing music lists? Do teachers have a responsibility to find out about many subject matters, musics, cultures—and then structure those subject matters for their students? Is there more freedom, more spontaneity if you do not know? If you just choose to ignore that there are 50 flavors, does that grant more freedom and is that somehow better than if you learn to organize the curriculum and plan? Does lack of awareness provide more freedom because it is more spontaneous and includes fewer available choices? No? Yes? Some people say, "If I think about it and I become aware then somehow it is not as valid." Is it somehow more sincere to teach your students only that which *you* learned in growing up?

What about the teacher who says, "Well, you cannot really teach anything to those kids because every child must learn for himself." This is somewhat frightening to hear because the teacher is discounting history. Must we make every mistake of the preceding generations again and again? Or is it possible for us to improve? Technology seems to be improving; we know that we do not have to invent the wheel again and again—the next person just keeps pushing it. We can extend technology from one generation to the next. But consider interpersonal relationships. Some would say that in interpersonal relationships we cannot learn except directly. It is suggested that, if at all possible, one should try to teach students to learn vicariously —at least concerning the consequences of bad things. This may be the major hope for our civilization. Must a child experience the hurt of prejudicial acts to understand how it feels to be discriminated against? Is it necessary for students to assault one another in order to learn about cruelty? Is it necessary for every generation to have war in order to learn the futility of war? Can some lessons be learned vicariously and spare humanity the pain of repetition?

You are preparing to teach children. What are you learning in that preparation? Can you teach children what you do not know? If there are 50 flavors and you know 10, then that is what you know. Unless you can get students into an ice cream store (library perhaps) that provides more flavors than you know, then your students will learn only 10 flavors. As the teacher you are the one who is running the store most of the time. These considerations represent very hard issues. They are what teaching is all about. Answers to such questions are not easy.

Once we have decided what we want—as teachers, parents, friends —then we can employ the techniques to go about achieving our goals and objectives. The techniques can deal with 3 flavors of ice cream, 50 flavors of ice cream, ice cream or no ice cream, spontaneity, lack of spontaneity, and most other things—if that is what we have decided we want. Before the teacher employs any teaching strategy, value choices ought to be made. Sometimes, it is indeed frightening to contemplate these values. The resultant power teachers have over students may be even more frightening. It seems many teachers are becoming more and more effective. It also seems that nobody will ever truly get upset with teachers until teachers can honestly prove that they are effective. It seems that no one has ever been too upset with muddling bungling teachers, but now that the profession is getting to the point where learning is insured, there seem to be more "gut level" reactions from people.

Being an effective teacher represents an immense responsibility. Jesus was an effective teacher, as was Socrates, and perhaps even Hitler. Teachers teach constantly whether or not they realize it. In the same manner students learn continuously. Teaching/learning goes on constantly, for example, if a teacher reacts to a certain type of music or does not react—if there is any reaction at all. A teacher may go into a school where there are an equal number of black and white children and the teacher touches all the black youngsters but not the white children, or vice versa, yet the teacher may not realize it. The teacher is not aware it is happening. What lesson (unintended) is taught and/or learned? Some teachers go so far as to say "I am not indoctrinating my values or my prejudices in my classroom." But of course they are, by the way they attend to, by the way they look at, by the way they do or do not accept differences of opinion, by every academic product or process, by their smile, by the look on their face.

The point is not that it is wrong for teachers to impose values. It is only wrong for teachers to go into classrooms and interact with children while imposing values that are unintentional and not given to thought, yet actually in their own mind believing that they are not imposing any values—that children are deciding all things for themselves. How often do we exist in our own stereotypes without being aware of them? Recall at this point the discussion about creativity and the one about embarrassment? Do such situations arise because those teachers were mean, vicious, or spiteful? Maybe occasionally, but it appears that most of them were well-intentioned people just like us who, perhaps, did not know, who may have trounced all over feelings yet did not even realize it because they were unaware—it was not in their routine.

Structure begins when one enters a classroom. As soon as people get together, even under a tree, structure begins. When they start talking we have even more structure. If it rains and we build a shelter to get in out of the rain even more structure emerges. And if there are too many people to meet all in the same room then other kinds of structure arise. Structure starts as soon as two people get together and continues as people continue. The crucial point is that some people persist in talking about unstructured education when they ought to be thinking about *how much* and *what kind* of structure. Others argue about imposing values or not imposing values when they should argue about *which values* to impose.

Many times we hear statements such as "Give me some techniques to make my room more quiet." "Give me some techniques to make my room less quiet." More participation, more freedom, and more thought is needed. Less participation, more freedom, and more thought is needed. "I realize that I only know seven flavors of ice cream, but that is perfectly all right with me because I have only three of them up there on my bookshelf and my principal does not bother me about it anyway. So I am just doing this because I *have to.*" The point is not whether we should impart values; the point is that we *do* impart them and we ought to be extremely careful about which ones we impart. Those little people are indeed learning from us, and it is frightening to realize they are learning exactly what we teach them *whether or not we think that is what we are teaching.* So . . .

Why are you here?
  You choose to be.

Why more than desire?
  Desire is not enough.

Why should you teach?
  To share some social, musical, and academic values.

Why music?
It is an extremely important part of our culture.

Who selects?
You do sometimes, with help from students.

Who can choose?
Those who have been taught to choose.

Who should participate?
Everyone initially, fewer later on.

Who is responsible?
You, the teacher; you, the student.

What is acculturation?
Bringing the student into the mainstream of his culture.

What is our subject matter?
Music, the standard curriculum and whatever else is important.

What is extra-musical?
Music not for its own sake.

What is creativity?
The reorganization of past experiences, at least in so far as it can
be taught.

When is today?
Always.

When is too soon?
Before the student is capable.

When is progress?
When it is observed.

When is independence?
Progressively, now and later.

How should teachers behave?
As they choose, even if it's not initially sincere.

How do teachers choose to act?
Approvingly, with firm procedures.

How important is structure?
Important enough to plan carefully.

How much good can we do?
A great deal!

TWO

SAMPLE LESSONS

The following sample lessons are designed to initiate undergraduate students into the teaching and learning of music subject matter. These lessons combine practical teaching experience with an opportunity to learn subject matter while participating as students in a laboratory situation. The authors encourage the use of elementary-age students in the laboratory–teaching class, but such a situation is usually the exception rather than the rule. Regardless, these sample lessons are intended as guides for practical teaching experience while simultaneously instructing subject matter which prospective classroom teachers can learn and teach with satisfaction and confidence. The lessons have been supervised and revised in classes over a 10-year period. The authors have found that students who have searched out their own illustrations and musical examples presented better lessons. For this reason exhaustive examples for concepts contained in each lesson have been avoided. In choosing examples to illustrate a particular concept it should be noted that perhaps every piece of music may represent most of the concepts therein discussed. Therefore, several examples of each objective should be given to ensure that students discriminate. Since the amount and scope of materials included in this text have been intentionally limited, persons using these lessons with children are encouraged to include many additional materials from school libraries, audio-visual material, basal series texts, popular recordings, and personal libraries. Such supplementation usually generates more enthusiasm (and learning) for all concerned (see Part III).

Considering the musical exposure which children acquire from electronic media (television, radio, movies, and records), it is apparent that by the time students enter school they have *experienced* and *discriminated* many musical sounds; therefore, a main purpose in the teaching of listening skills might be to help students *associate* verbal labels with musical sounds. It must be remembered that much musical understanding exists on a non-verbal level. Regardless, in directed listening activities students can be instructed to listen for something specific each time a piece is presented.

In an actual teaching situation with children, the sample lesson format presented in this text may comprise only a portion of a complete lesson, or the teacher may choose to isolate only one aspect or concept if the lesson is long. More review and opportunity for performance demonstration of learning may be necessary, and other activities, such as the performance of familiar songs through singing and playing instruments may be included to balance the range of activities and musical experiences to which students are exposed. Also, many activities can be included for pure listening and performing enjoyment.

When using these lessons with university classes the authors have had each student in the class write a short description of what was learned at the conclusion of every lesson. Video taping presentations also have been effective in helping prospective teachers gain insight into how they function in the teaching role. Also, advanced students sometimes present the lessons in the style of Kodaly, Orff, Mannhattanville, and so on. Having students in the class write a short critique of the lesson presentation, listing four good things each teacher did and suggesting one area for improvement has also been effective. This teaches the *evaluator* how to find positive aspects of performance. Outlines for the musical evaluation and teaching evaluation of each teacher are included for reference. (See Exhibits 1 and 2.)

EXHIBIT 1

MUSICAL EVALUATION

TEACHER _____

EVALUATOR _____

(Rate each blank 1 through 10; 1 is low, 10 is high)

Did the teacher seem well prepared and familiar with the material used?   ____

Were the teacher's musical intentions clearly conveyed through the presentation?   ____

Was the teacher able to identify and deal with important musical problems? Rate items below that are either very good or need improvement.

Intonation____ Tone quality ____ Breathing ____ Consonants   ____
Tempo   ____ Vowels   ____ Rhythm   ____ Phrasing   ____
Ensemble ____ Balance   ____ Dynamics____ Posture   ____

Did the teacher work toward improvement of musicianship and musical understanding?   ____

Did the teacher present creatively or attempt to stimulate student creativity?   ____

What suggestions would you offer for the development of the teacher's musical presentation?

_____

_____

EXHIBIT 2

TEACHING EVALUATION

TEACHER _____

EVALUATOR _____

(Rate each blank 1 through 10; 1 is low, 10 is high)

Did the teacher seem well prepared and familiar with the material used? _____

Were the verbal instructions given by the teacher clear, concise, and easily heard? _____

Did the teacher's approach to the group encourage you to give your best efforts? _____

Did the teacher present creatively or attempt to stimulate student creativity? _____

Did the teacher make effective use of teaching aids and materials? _____

How many times did the teacher approve/disapprove of student social and academic behavior?　Approve _____

Disapprove_____

List four positive things the teacher did.

_____

_____

List one suggestion for improvement.

_____

The following suggestions are presented to help students make the most effective use of these lessons*:

1.   Read the objective for the lesson carefully and form an idea of the concept(s) to be taught.

2.   Read the procedures section, familiarizing yourself with the methodology required to teach the concept.

3.   Read the evaluation section. Usually the evaluation of a lesson will require students to transfer their learning of a concept to different examples which are similar to those used in the lesson procedures.

4.   Reread the objective and procedure sections.

5.   Read other texts and source materials or consult with your instructor for explanations and musical examples to use in your lesson.

6.   Collect and prepare materials and/or musical examples for your presentation.

7.   Develop an evaluation technique to assess student learning.

8.   Most important: Make the lesson interesting to your students.

After this sequence of lessons has been completed in elementary music methods classes taught by the authors, students prepare and teach original lessons. They are instructed to (1) specify a lesson objective, (2) choose musical examples, (3) decide upon teaching procedures, (4) structure teacher-student interactions to reinforce acquisition of subject matter and appropriate social behaviors, and (5) devise evaluative criteria to assess student learning.

*We would like to thank Gene M. Simons, University of Georgia, for developing the model lessons from which the following were adapted.

SAMPLE LESSONS

1. UNACCOMPANIED ROTE SONG*

OBJECTIVE

Students will teach the class a short unaccompanied rote song.

PROCEDURES

Each student selects a short song or portion of a longer song to teach the class within a time limit of 5 minutes.

In teaching a song by rote one provides a model which students can imitate. The teacher works toward musical singing, that is, expressiveness with accuracy in pitches and rhythms. The students do not have printed music, although the words may be written out. Always make sure students are given a starting pitch before they begin singing.

EVALUATION

The class will sing the selection without aid from the teacher.

*Each student in the class presents these lessons.

2. ACCOMPANIED ROTE SONG

OBJECTIVE

Students will teach the class a short accompanied rote song.

PROCEDURES

Students will teach a short rote song while accompanying the class using melodic or harmonic instruments. Each lesson should be limited to 5 minutes.

EVALUATION

The class will sing the rote song while the teacher accompanies on an instrument.

3. DYNAMICS: RECOGNIZING LOUD AND SOFT

OBJECTIVE

Students will verbally describe and perform three ways in which the dynamics of a piece of music can be controlled.

PROCEDURES

Dynamics have to do with the loudness and softness of music and give variety and expression to music.

Read a poem to the class without changing the dynamic level. Then read it again with dynamic expression to demonstrate dynamic contrasts in speech.

The following symbols are used in musical notation to indicate dynamics: *pp* (very soft), *p* (soft), *mp* (moderately soft), *mf* (moderately loud), *f* (loud), *ff* (very loud).

Students will verbally describe three ways dynamic changes can be produced in a class performance of a song: (1) vary number of singers, (2) singers vary intensity level (loudness), and (3) add or delete accompanying instruments at appropriate sections of the song.

EVALUATION

Students will sing a song employing dynamic contrasts indicated in the musical score. Dynamic contrasts will be produced in the three ways indicated above.

4. DYNAMICS: INSTRUMENTAL CONTRASTS

OBJECTIVE

Students will perform a song demonstrating understanding of dynamic markings found in printed music.

PROCEDURES

Play a portion of a piece of music and ask one student to verbally describe the dynamics of the piece including whether the piece contained few or many dynamic contrasts. Continuing to listen to the piece, students may show dynamic changes by having arms outstretched for loud passages. Mention that conductors often indicate dynamic changes by the size of their conducting patterns.

Students will indicate if dynamics were changed by varying

1. types of instruments/voices

2. number of instruments/voices

3. intensity of the same types and numbers of instruments/voices

4. distance between sound source and listener

To demonstrate that dynamics are not just soft or loud but are continuous from very soft to very loud, have a student play an instrument beginning softly and gradually becoming louder. In addition, the entire class can crescendo and diminuendo while singing a song (get gradually louder and gradually softer). The musical symbols for increases and decreases in sound intensity are crescendo (<) and diminuendo (>).

EVALUATION

Play another selection and ask students to describe the dynamics at cued places in the music using the words softest, soft, loud, and loudest. Students should also describe how the dynamic changes were made.

5. TONE COLOR: DIFFERENTIATING MUSICAL SOUNDS

OBJECTIVE

Students will identify specific tone colors in recorded examples.

PROCEDURES

The following outline provides a suggested organization for many lessons. It is recommended that the teacher sensitize students to tone color in conjunction with every music lesson by teaching students to discriminate and verbally identify all musical sounds encountered.

I. Vocal
   A. Female (adult)
      1. Soprano
      2. Alto
      3. Contralto
   B. Male (adult)
      1. Contratenor
      2. Tenor
      3. Baritone
      4. Bass
   C. Child

II. Instrumental
   A. Unfretted string
      1. Violin
      2. Viola
      3. Cello
      4. String Bass

B. Fretted string
   1. Guitar
   2. Lute
   3. Banjo
   4. Mandolin
   5. Dulcimer
C. Woodwind
   1. Flute/Piccolo/Recorder
   2. Oboe/English horn
   3. Clarinet
   4. Bassoon
   5. Saxophone
D. Brass
   1. Trumpet/Cornet
   2. French horn
   3. Trombone
   4. Tuba
   5. Sousaphone
E. Keyboard
   1. Piano
   2. Organ
   3. Harpsichord
   4. Celesta
F. Percussion
   1. Kettledrums (tympani)
   2. Bass/Snare drum
   3. Cymbals
   4. Tambourine
   5. Woodblock
   6. Triangle
G. Electronic
   1. Synthesizer
   2. Electric guitar
   3. Electronic piano
   4. Electronic organs

Many groups are identified by the tone colors contained: Chorus (vocal), Band (woodwind, brass, percussion), Orchestra (unfretted strings, woodwind, brass, percussion), String Quartet (two violins, viola, cello), and so on.

EVALUATION

Students will identify tone colors in musical examples. Two pieces written to demonstrate tone color are *Peter and the Wolf* by Prokofiev and *Young Person's Guide to the Orchestra* by Britten.

6. TONE COLOR: THE RELATION OF PITCH AND DYNAMICS

OBJECTIVE

Students will identify instrument timbres when performed at varying pitch and dynamic levels.

PROCEDURES

1. Pitch and dynamic levels are relative for each instrument.

2. Dynamic levels may be affected by pitch levels for each instrument.

Availability of instruments and recordings will determine the presentation of this lesson.

These concepts may be introduced by the following brief discussion of range: Highness and lowness are relative to the instrument performing any particular tone. Middle C is a very low tone in the range of a flute; however, it is a very high tone in the range of a tuba. Middle C is in the middle range of the piano. The "range" of an instrument includes all the tones the instrument can play from its lowest to highest tone.

EVALUATION

Students will explore musical and environmental sounds to compare the effect of pitch and dynamic levels on timbre.

Examples such as the beginning of "Til Eulenspiegel" (French horn) by R. Strauss may be played for identification and discussion.

7. PITCH: REORGANIZING HIGH AND LOW

OBJECTIVE

Students will identify high and low pitches, defining pitch as the highness and lowness of sounds.

PROCEDURES

Have students sing (on "ooh") ascending glissandi to experience singing from low pitches to high pitches. Repeat using descending glissandi.

Play a few notes of any scale several times up and down, having students indicate with their hands (gradually up and down) as the pitch gets higher and lower. Repeat this exercise, with students closing their eyes as they indicate the rise and fall of the pitch.

Students will indicate which of two presented tones is lower, higher, or if they are the same. Remind students that musical tones have qualities other than loudness and softness.

Given a pitched instrument (tone bells or piano), students will perform tones in the following pitch relationships (H = high, L = low): H-L, L-H, H-H (same), L-L (same).

EVALUATION

1. Students will notate the pitch contour of three and four-note melodies using line notation. For instance

As performed   As notated by students

2. Pick a song the students know quite well and have them write the pitches of the first five tones in line notation.

8. PITCH: DESCRIBING MELODIC CONTOUR

OBJECTIVE

Students will graphically describe the melodic contour of familiar songs.

PROCEDURES

Melodic contour is the *shape* of the intervals as pitches follow one another. Graphic description of melodic contour focuses attention on the rise and fall of a melodic line and is preparatory to the introduction of staff notation. Students should be made conscious of the aural-visual relationship of notes that are the same, move up, or move down. This may be described in several ways.

For example:

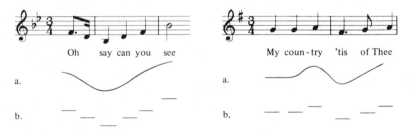

"Clementine" may be described by each student in this way.

EVALUATION

Students will describe the melodic contour of a familiar tune. Given five titles of familiar tunes, students will select the appropriate graphic description from five examples.

9. PITCH: IDENTIFYING STAFF NOTATION

OBJECTIVE

Students will identify letter names of notes on the treble clef staff and relate the notated pitches to aural and visual descriptions of melodic contour.

PROCEDURES

To show the rise and fall of pitches, a staff is used. It is a set of five lines and four spaces (ledger lines may be added) upon which notes are written. For identification, the first seven letters of the alphabet are used. The names of the notes on the lines and spaces are determined by the clef which appears at the beginning of each staff.

The most common clef is the treble or G clef, which identifies the second line (counted from the bottom) as G above middle C on the piano. Pianists will use two staffs with notes named by the treble and bass clefs. There are other clefs.

Treble Clef   Bass Clef

         G   B

Music is written this way for all voices and almost all instruments. By remembering the names of the spaces, F-A-C-E, the staff names are easily learned.

(D)   E   F   G   A   B   C   D   E   F   (G)

EVALUATION

1. Given a musical staff students will label the letter names of the lines and spaces.

2. Students will write the following words in pitch notation using half notes (𝅗𝅥) on a treble staff to indicate letters: DAD, FADE, CAFE, CAGE, GAB, BAG, BED, CABBAGE.

10. PITCH: PERFORMING FROM STAFF NOTATION

OBJECTIVE

Students will perform melodies written in staff notation on melodic percussion instruments or the keyboard.

PROCEDURES

By identifying the names of the notes on the staff and finding the corresponding note on a musical instrument, it is possible to play a tune which is written, that is, to read music.

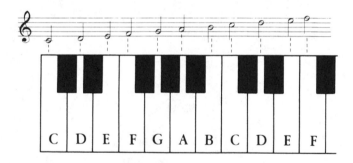

Students should be given several familiar tunes or melodic fragments for performance. The following examples use white notes only. Although the time values of notes may not have been discussed, it is suggested that they be included. This may increase transference of the learning experience to practical situations.

EVALUATION

Students will write in the names of the notes in the following examples. By sounding the notes, students will identify the tunes and write in the names above the staff. This activity may be done in small groups.

Name of Tune   _____

Name of Tune   _____

Name of Tune   _____

11. PITCH: RECOGNIZING KEYBOARD LETTER NAMES

OBJECTIVE

Students will identify letter names of piano keys.

Each white key has a letter name from A through G. Students will identify groups of two and three black keys as an aid in identifying white key names. By establishing that D is the white note between each set of two black notes, students can find all other notes.

Students will identify half-steps as being the pitch distance between two adjacent keys. Most half steps occur between a white and a black key. Two exceptions are the half steps between E–F and B–C, both of which occur between white keys.

Black keys do not have independent letter names. They are named in relation to an adjacent white key using a sharp or a flat. A sharp (#) placed with a letter indicates the key one-half step higher than the white key; whereas, a flat (♭) placed with a letter indicates the key one-half step lower than the white key. All notes on the keyboard have at least two names; these are called *enharmonic names*. That is, F# is the enharmonic name for G♭.

EVALUATION

1. Given an unlabeled keyboard students will perform isolated pitches when given letter names of keys verbally.

2. Using the materials in the evaluation of Lesson 8, students will perform simple melodies from staff notation.

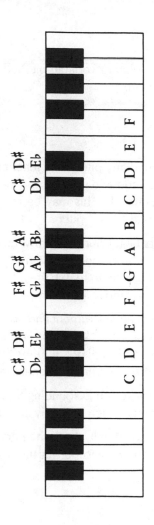

12. PITCH: TUNING AN INSTRUMENT

OBJECTIVE

Students will indicate when a variable-pitched instrument is in tune with a comparison pitch.

PROCEDURES

Have one student sound any pitch. The teacher then sounds several pitches or sings a glissando and students indicate when the student's and teacher's pitches match. This may be repeated, with a student approximating a second "first" pitch.

Have all the students begin humming any note. Then ask them to slide or glissando until everyone is humming the same pitch. Ask students what they had to do to match the pitch. (Some had to move higher and some had to move lower in pitch.)

"In tune" means that every instrument and voice is sounding as close to its proper pitch as possible. Why is it important for musicians to tune their instruments and to play "in tune?" "In tune" instruments and voices sound more pleasing to listeners in our musical culture.

An instrument or voice which is sounding below its "proper" pitch is said to be *flat,* and that which is slightly above is considered *sharp.*

Given a guitar, one student will match the pitch of each string to the proper notes on a piano or another (in tune) guitar.

EVALUATION

Ask students (1) to define verbally what is meant by "in tuneness," and (2) to tune one (out-of-tune) string on a guitar.

13. DURATION: IDENTIFYING THE BEAT

OBJECTIVE

Students will identify the beat in musical examples.

PROCEDURES

Students will define beats as points in time/space separated by *equal* durations. One beat cannot exist alone; there must be more than one point for the phenomenon to manifest itself. If the durations between beats are equal, then beats must be steady. This concept may be represented visually as follows:

Clap your hands once and ask students if that was an example of steady beat. (No.) Have students identify, by raising hands (with eyes closed), examples of beats:

1. clap erratic unsteady pattern (no)

2. clap fast steady pattern (yes)

3. clap slow unsteady pattern (no)

4. clap slow steady pattern (yes)

Ask students to name common things that produce a steady beat (clock, metronome, heart, pulse, sprinkler).

Have two students demonstrate unsteady beat by clapping. Make sure students clap unsteady beats (unequal) not different rhythms within a steady beat.

Have students clap a steady beat.

Students will clap the beat as they sing a song with a steady beat.

In much music with a regular pulse (a steady beat), people perceive strong beats and weaker beats. Throughout the above song a strong beat is followed by a weaker beat. This may be described graphically.

EVALUATION

Students will clap and/or march to the beat of recorded musical selections. Marches make good musical materials for this activity as they have a strong pulse. The teacher should be certain that all students move precisely with the beat of the music.

Students will identify selected listening examples as having a steady or unsteady beat, differentiate between music which has a driving pulse, that is, where the beat is very marked, and music which is less marked, that is, where the pulse is more subtle, causing the music to flow more easily.

14. DURATION: RECOGNIZING BEAT SUBDIVISION

OBJECTIVE

Students will define beat subdivision as the combination of several *equal* shorter notes into the duration of one beat and will write the first and second subdivisions for plain and dotted beat note values.

PROCEDURES

Explain that beat notes subdivide into first and second subdivisions as given in the chart below:

BEAT NOTE VALUE	FIRST SUBDIVISION OF BEAT NOTE	SECOND SUBDIVISION OF BEAT NOTE
Plain note = Twoness	Two equal notes in duration of one beat	Four equal notes in duration of one beat
half		
quarter		
eighth		
Dotted note = Threeness	Three equal notes in duration of one beat	Six equal notes in duration of one beat
half		
quarter		
eighth		

EVALUATION

1. Students will write the first subdivision of selected beat note values.

2. Students will sing one verse of several songs from a basal text, define the beat by clapping softly, determine what notational value is receiving one beat, and indicate if that beat notational value subdivides into twoness or threeness. The teacher must be sure that the note value indicated by a student is actually the value receiving the beat. Many songs can be performed with two different notational values as the beat note value.

15. DURATION: RECOGNIZING TEMPO, THE RATE OF THE BEAT

OBJECTIVE

Students will suggest tempo for selected songs by clapping.

PROCEDURES

Tempo is the rate of the steady beat. It is more precisely defined by using a metronome to indicate the number of steady beats per minute. Tempo can change by slowing down (ritardando) or speeding up (accelerando).

In establishing tempo for a notated piece of music, a particular note value represents the duration of the beat. This beat tempo is represented in printed music by a symbol indicating the beat note value and the metronomic speed at which the piece should move. For instance, ♩ = 84 indicates that a quarter note will receive one beat at a tempo of 84 beats per minute.

The teacher should select a familiar song to sing, then have the group tap the steady beat while singing it a second time. Maintaining this steady beat, use the metronome to identify the beat note rate. This exercise may be repeated with a song of contrasting tempo.

After identifying the beat note value students will use a metronome to establish a slow, moderate, and fast tempo for the following song (♩ = 50, 84, 120). Be certain that the quarter note remains the beat note value in this demonstration.

There was a farm-er had a dog and Bin-go was his name - o B I

N G O B I N G O B I N G O and Bin-go was his name - o.

This song may be sung substituting claps for letters in the following manner:

(1) B I N G O
(2) x I N G O
(3) x x N G O
(4) x x x G O
(5) x x x x O
(6) x x x x x

EVALUATION

The class will sing *Bingo* beginning at a tempo of ♩ = 60. Each repeat will be taken at a faster tempo. Listen to the last movement of *Toy Symphony*. Does each repeat of the melody go faster or slower than the preceding rendition of the melody?

16. DURATION: DIFFERENTIATING RHYTHM, THE DIVISIONS OF THE BEAT

OBJECTIVE

Students will differentiate the division(s) of beat(s) by (1) identifying rhythmic patterns from a chart, and (2) notating patterns heard.

PROCEDURES

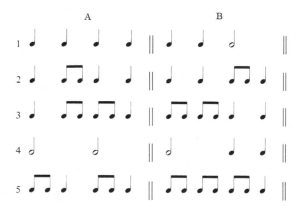

From a clear chart, the teacher will clap either A or B for each example. Students should repeat the pattern and identify it, noting aural and visual comparisons for each example. Next the teacher may select any one of the ten examples for performance and identification. Students should also select and perform for their peers. All performers should aim toward a steady pulse.

Dictation may be introduced by having students identify and copy selected measures clapped by the teacher.

In this lesson, aural-visual cognition is considered of primary importance. Vocabulary (1/4 notes, 1/2 notes, 1/8 notes, etc.) may be introduced for older students or students with some background in music; however, this is not considered vital at present.

EVALUATION

Students will write down a new example performed by the teacher using ♩ , ♩ , and  .

For example:

17. DURATION: RECOGNIZING METER, THE GROUPING OF THE BEATS

OBJECTIVE

Students will aurally identify musical examples of metric groupings in two (duple), three (triple), four (quadruple), five (quintuple), and so on.

PROCEDURES

All music with regular (steady) pulse moves in some form of two and three groups; that is, 4 is twice two, $\frac{6}{8}$ is two or twice three, and so on. Beat *groupings* should not be confused with beat *divisions* (see lesson 14).

Emphasis should be placed on the students' need to find the first of the group, that is, "one," and thereafter attempt to decide if the grouping is 1–2 or 1–2–3. Students should clap on "one" and count the remainder as a recording is played.

By giving many short examples at varying tempi, practice is given in finding the first of a group. Movement to represent the grouping is encouraged, for example, $\frac{2}{2}$, $\frac{2}{4}$, $\frac{6}{8}$, knees-clap, $\frac{3}{4}$ knees-clap-clap, or step-clap-clap; $\frac{4}{4}$ knees-snap-clap-snap.

This chart of meters is included for the assistance of teachers only.

	SIMPLE Subdivision of beats is in two			COMPOUND Subdivision of beats is in three		
Duple (moves in two)	2 8	2 4	2 2	6 2	6 4	6 8
Triple (moves in three)	3 8	3 4	3 2	9 4	9 8	9 16
Quadruple (moves in four)	4 8	4 4	4 2	12 4	12 8	12 16

For example, $\frac{6}{8}$ is compound division of the beat (threeness) while the beats are most often grouped in twos. There are two dotted quarter notes, or the mathematical equivalent of two ♩. 's in a measure. This is duple *grouping* of the beats.

Each beat or dotted quarter note may be divided into three eighth notes (compound).

EVALUATION

Given five musical examples, students will identify beat groupings in each example. Students may suggest appropriate time-signatures.

18. DURATION: RHYTHM PERFORMANCE

OBJECTIVE

Students will perform a rhythm score by clapping or playing percussion instruments.

PROCEDURES

With independence a goal in music instruction, it is important to keep rhythm performance simple and with several parts being played simultaneously. However, at the outset, all students should perform each part. After success, the class may be divided into two groups. One group will clap and the other group will tap on chairs (books, with pencils, and so on). Following the same procedure, the groups may be changed and the third part added with a different "natural" sound.

The teacher should select a recorded example of music in $\frac{4}{4}$, $\frac{2}{4}$, $\frac{2}{2}$, meter which students may accompany using rhythm instruments. An example of a simple repeated, three-part percussion accompaniment is given.

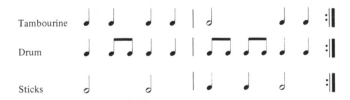

Use of a record allows the teacher to assist in maintaining a steady pulse and eye-contact with the music. Parts may be rotated, added to familiar songs, and extended.

Verbal associations have long been considered useful in reading rhythms. Orff, Kodaly and others suggest verbalizing the rhythm. These can be extended to include any words in the student's world, for example, food, names of people, places, ball teams, or short phrases.

For example:

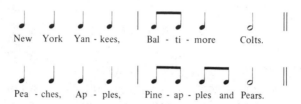

EVALUATION

1. Small groups (perhaps three persons to each part) will perform the example to recorded music.

2. Students will select a familiar song and suggest a two- or four-measure rhythmic pattern using ♩ , ♩ , and ♫ for a percussion accompaniment. The choice of instruments is determined by mood, number, and availability.

19. NOTATION: NAMING DURATION VALUES

OBJECTIVE

Students will identify longer and shorter note and rest durations by names.

PROCEDURES

Durational values of notes and rests are listed below from shortest to longest. A dot following a note or rest adds one-half the durational value to the symbol. For instance, a dotted half note (𝅗𝅥.) is equal to the duration of a half note plus a quarter note (𝅗𝅥 + ♩). Likewise, a dotted rest symbol is equal to the value of the symbol plus one-half the value of the symbol (𝄽· = 𝄽 + 𝄾).

Note Symbol	Rest Symbol	Durational Name
𝅘𝅥𝅯	𝄿	sixteenth (1/16)
♪	𝄾	eighth (1/8)
♩	𝄽	quarter (1/4)
𝅗𝅥	𝄼	half (1/2)
𝅝	𝄻	whole

The duration of each note and rest is always equal to the duration of two of the values immediately above that value in the chart:

(♩ = ♪ + ♪). This is also true if the notes are dotted (♩ = ♪. + ♪.). However, a dotted note can also be divided into *three* equal notes (♩. = ♪ + ♪ + ♪).

A chart illustrating the mathematical relationship of notes may be placed on a wall for easy reference during all subsequent lessons.

For example:

Name	Fraction	Rests			Notes	
whole note		𝄻			𝅝	
half note	1/2					
quarter note	1/4					
eighth note	1/8					
sixteenth note	1/16					

The value of the dot can be shown in the sequences which follow. Examples b and c will sound alike.

a.

b.

c.

a.

b.

c.

It is useful to relate ♩. ♪ to "My Country 'Tis of Thee," "O Beautiful for Spacious Skies" or "God of Our Fathers," and ♩♩ to "O Say Can You See," "The Battle Hymn of the Republic," or "Waltzing Matilda."

EVALUATION

Students will visually indicate the longest and shortest note and rest values in selected songs and identify the durational and pitch names of those notes.

20: NOTATION: SPECIFYING LONGNESS AND SHORTNESS BY LINE NOTATION

OBJECTIVE

Students will identify long and short tones in a melody and define duration as the longness and shortness of tones.

PROCEDURES

Sing a familiar song such as "Down in the Valley" with every note the same length. Ask students what was wrong with the melody. (The notes should not all last the same amount of time.) It should be noted that duration, dynamics, and pitch are independent elements of music. Any given tone can be loud or soft, high or low, short or long.

Students will notate the duration of three dictated tones in line notation. One student will notate at the board so answers can be checked after each example. Students should pay particular attention to representing duration by the length of the lines and pitch by the height of the lines. Music notation is a picture of the way the music goes: pitch

As performed by teacher   As notated by students

has to do with highness and lowness of tones, and duration has to do with shortness and longness of tones.

EVALUATION

Students will notate the pitch and duration of the first five tones of a familiar song in line notation. Is the line notation written by each student an accurate "picture of the way the music sounds?"

21. NOTATION: COUNTING RHYTHMIC DIVISIONS

OBJECTIVES

Students will write in the counting for the melodic rhythm of a song notated in ⁴₄ which contains only half, quarter, and eighth notes.

PROCEDURES

In counting rhythm each beat may be represented by a number. In the following ⁴₄ metric time each beat is represented by a quarter note; therefore, the quarter note beat values each receive a count:

Half notes, which are equal to two quarter notes, would each receive two beats:

Eighth notes, two of which are equal to one quarter note, would be played two per beat and are counted as follows:

EVALUATION

Students will write in the counting for the following rhythms.

Students will write in the counting for the following melodic rhythm.

22: NOTATION: RHYTHMIC PERFORMANCE INCLUDING
o and ⸰

OBJECTIVE

Students will (1) identify rhythm patterns from a chart, (2) perform a rhythm score, and/or write in the counting for the melodic rhythm including the whole note (o) and the quarter rest (⸰).

PROCEDURES

A whole note represents one sound held for the equivalent time value of 4 quarter notes, 2 half notes, or 8 eighth notes. A quarter rest represents silence for the equivalent time value of one quarter note. Where percussion instruments are used it is necessary to establish the difference in the sound of

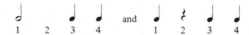

The sound of the half note continues to the next quarter note, that is, continues to the count on three. The sound of the quarter note in the second example extends to the rest, that is, it is stopped on the second count.

These concepts should be introduced to reinforce the sequence outlined in lesson 19 and also identified in songs.

EVALUATION

Evaluation may follow the suggestions given for Lessons, 10, 20 and 21.

Students will clap the following rhythm while the melody of "Early One Morning" is played.

23. NOTATION: AURAL DICTATION

OBJECTIVE

Students will notate simple rhythms from aural dictation.

PROCEDURES

Review: A beat can be notated as either a plain or a dotted note value. A plain note subdivides into two equal shorter note values and a dotted note subdivides into three equal shorter note values.

After four aural presentations students will notate the following rhythmic examples using only plain or dotted quarter notes to represent the beat note value and eighth notes to represent first subdivisions. Have students listen carefully and decide if beats subdivide into twoness or threeness. If the subdivisions are in twoness then beat note values will be plain. If subdivisions are in threeness the beat values will be dotted. Give students feedback after each example:

EVALUATION

Students will notate the following rhythms from aural dictation.

24. NOTATION: NOTATING STACCATO AND LEGATO STYLE

OBJECTIVE

Students will identify and perform examples of staccato and legato style.

PROCEDURES

The same notational value may be performed either staccato (crisp, short) or legato (practically connected, full durational value). In performing staccato style the durational value is shortened approximately one-half and the remainder of the beat is considered a rest. The mark for staccato is a dot above or below the note ahead. Notes to be played legato are joined by a slur.

Play several recorded examples and have the class indicate whether the style is staccato or legato. Have the students notate through aural dictation staccato and legato patterns.

EVALUATION

1. Students will sing songs in both styles and suggest places for inclusion of both legato and staccato articulation in a selected song.

2. Students will listen to several performed or recorded examples of staccato and legato style, identify these, and give notation for both styles (for example, pizzicato in string playing).

25. MODE: CONSTRUCTING MAJOR SCALES

OBJECTIVE

Students will relate the familiar sound of a major scale to staff notation and the keyboard and perform this ascending and descending.

PROCEDURES

A scale is a series of pitches arranged in an order which is constant for each type of scale. The familiar sound of the major scale (*do, re, me, fa, sol, la, ti, do*) may be produced by playing C and the white notes above it until the next C. This succession of notes is called a C major scale. Students will sing/perform this pattern of notes using a neutral vowel, numbers (that is, 1–2–3–4) and solfege (*do, re, me*).

Beginning on G, the students will identify the one note which changes the sound of the major scale. It is F and must be changed to F# in order to maintain the constant relationship of tones and semi-tones in a major scale.

If the scale is begun on F, students will identify the "wrong" note as being B and change this to B♭.

These accidentals, that is, sharps and flats, which change selected notes to produce a major (or minor) scale are placed at the beginning of each staff and are called key signatures. From this one can state the key (or *do*) in which the melody is written. The key signatures for major scales are different from those for minor scales.

Some major scale key signatures are:

E♭   B♭   F   C   G   D   A   E

EVALUATION

Students will aurally identify notes which must be altered when the major scale is begun on D. Students will write the key signatures for the keys discussed and be able to explain each one.

26. MODE: RECOGNIZING KEY SIGNATURES/ACCIDENTALS

OBJECTIVE

Students will identify and perform notes affected by key signatures and accidentals.

PROCEDURES

The key signature (sharps or flats at the beginning of each staff) indicates letter names which are sharped or flatted throughout the entire composition. For instance, a sharp on the F line of the staff in a key signature requires that all the Fs in the song be raised a half step to F#.

Accidentals are sharps (#), flats (♭), or naturals (♮) which occur within a composition. They affect only the single pitch which they precede and they affect all notes on that pitch until the next bar line or until another accidental alters that same pitch. Sharps raise a tone one half-step; flats lower a tone one half-step; and naturals cancel sharps and flats.

Given several selections from songs, students will indicate which notes are affected by key signatures and accidentals.

Four students will perform the six-pitch examples below using tone bells so all members of the class can hear and see the performances:

EVALUATION

Students will perform the pitches in the "Coventry Carol" on bells.

27. MODE: IDENTIFYING PENTATONIC SCALES

OBJECTIVE

Students will aurally identify pentatonic scales and musical examples as being in major or pentatonic mode.

PROCEDURE

The prefix "penta" means "five"; a pentatonic scale has five notes within an octave. There are several possible arrangements of intervals constituting pentatonic scales. These are easily observed by starting on any black note on the keyboard and playing successive black notes to the octave. Tonal relationships most frequently heard are those which begin on F# and/or C#.

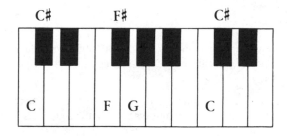

A pentatonic scale is easily transposed to white notes by playing a major scale (a) without the fourth and seventh degrees, or (b) without the third and seventh degrees. (This deletion eliminates semi-tones in the scale.)

a. Pentatonic scales starting   b. Pentatonic scales starting on G
   on C

or   or

Carl Orff's *Schulwerk* is based upon this scale. Its versatility in providing simple improvisatory experiences for students is recognized in most methods texts and basal series. The teacher is encouraged to investigate these.

Some familiar songs in the pentatonic mode are listed in the indices of basal series texts.

EVALUATION

1. Students will (a) sing and/or aurally identify major and pentatonic scales, and (b) identify musical examples as being in major or pentatonic mode.

2. Students will perform music with a melody line and simple repetitive rhythmic/melodic accompaniments (ostinati) using notes from the pentatonic scale.

28. MODE: DIFFERENTIATING MAJOR AND MINOR

OBJECTIVE

Students will aurally identify musical examples as being in major or minor mode.

PROCEDURES

Mode is determined by the scale within which the melody's notes are found and by the chords which accompany the melody. The major scale (Lesson 25) should be briefly reviewed. There are several forms of a minor scale. Although other notes (sixth and seventh degrees of scale) are sometimes altered, the third note is always lowered one semi-tone. Referring to the example of C major and C minor, the student should be made aware of the difference in the third degree of the scale.

This change in the relationship of tones and semi-tones causes a difference in the sound of the primary triads.

The effect of the flattened third degree is obvious in the major and minor versions of the first line of "Mary Had a Little Lamb."

Comparison of the first and third verses of "Raindrops on Roses" may be used to illustrate the contrast of minor-major harmony on a constant melody line.

For each major scale, there is a relative minor scale. These two scales will have the same key-signature. The relative minor scale is found by counting down three notes from the first note of the major scale. For example, C major has no sharps or flats; to find the minor scale which has no sharps or flats, count down three notes from C to A: the relative major scale of A minor is, therefore, C major.

Some relative keys and their key-signatures and key-notes are given below:

F maj. D min.   C maj. A min.   G maj. E min.   D maj. B min.

These relationships are evident in songs which modulate within major and minor keys, for example, "Greensleeves," "Erie Canal," "We Three Kings." Much music of the Romantic period illustrates this relationship of major and minor keys.

The teacher will either perform songs or play recordings for the class which illustrate major and minor mode. Each example or recorded section should be fairly short. Basal series recordings make a good source for this lesson.

Examples should not confound other musical elements with mode. For instance, all minor examples should not be slow, low pitched, and played on string instruments. Several examples should be presented which keep one mode while changing other elements. Then a few examples of the other mode should be presented, illustrating different elements while keeping mode constant.

132

EVALUATION

Play three songs, each in major and minor mode. Have students identify the mode of each of the six examples. "Twinkle, Twinkle Little Star," "Aunt Rhody," and "Joshua" make good examples for this assessment.

29. HARMONY: IDENTIFYING INTERVALS

OBJECTIVE

Students will aurally identify intervals played melodically or harmonically and identify notated examples.

PROCEDURES

Students will define *interval* as the pitch distance between two tones. The name of an interval indicates the number of staff lines and spaces included between two tones. That is, the size of an interval is found by counting the number of letter names included.

The interval F to the F above (or below) is called an *octave* because it includes eight pitches (F, G, A, B, C, D, E, F). Two identical pitches (G, G) form an interval known as the *unison*. The interval G to the B above it includes the notes G, A, and B and, therefore, is called a *third* because it includes three notes. These are illustrated below.

octave   unison   3rd

This discussion refers to intervals based upon the key-note of major scales. The order of presentation is recommended for all groups.

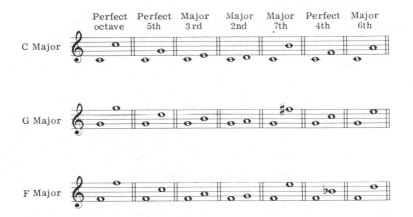

The sound of an interval may be identified by memorizing, by associating the two notes with the first two notes of a familiar song, or by mentally singing and counting intervening notes. It is suggested that the teacher give examples of all three approaches.

For example:

Major 7th	discordant sound
Perfect 5th	violins tuning
Major 6th	"My Bonnie Lies Over the Ocean"
Perfect 4th	"Auld Lang Syne"
Major 2nd	counting notes
Major 3rd	counting notes

All intervals are qualified. If the upper note is in the major scale of the lower note, unisons, octaves, fourths and fifths are called *perfect,* and seconds, thirds, sixths, and sevenths are called *major.* (Refer to above examples.)

For example, in the key of C, an F is usually played. The interval from C to F would be a *perfect* fourth. By placing a sharp in front of the F, the interval size is increased and it becomes augmented.

Where intervals are decreased in size by one half-step, *major* intervals become *minor,* and *perfect* intervals become *diminished.*

For example:

| major
7th | minor
7th | | perfect
5th | diminished
5th |

Increased by 1/2-step						*augmented*		
Interval size	unison	2nd	3rd	4th	5th	6th	7th	octave
Upper note within scale of lower note	perf.	maj.	maj.	perf.	perf.	maj.	maj.	perf.
Decreased by 1/2-step	dim.	min.	min.	dim.	dim.	min.	min.	dim.

EVALUATION

Students will aurally identify intervals played melodically (that is, one note after the other) and harmonically (two notes played simultaneously) and identify notated examples in the keys of C, F, and G.

30. HARMONY: SELECTING APPROPRIATE CHORDS FOR ACCOMPANIMENT

OBJECTIVE

Students suggest appropriate places for chord changes and select chords (using I, IV, and V chords) for a familiar song.

PROCEDURES

Harmony is created by the simultaneous sounding of two or more pitches. The most commonly used chords or combinations of pitches in major and minor keys are those built upon the first, fourth, and fifth degrees of a scale.

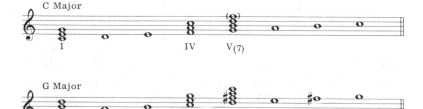

In C major, these primary chords are: I—CEG; IV—FAC; and V—GBD. In G Major, the chords are: I—GBD; IV—CEG; and V—DF#A. A seventh may be added to the chord on V, for example, GBDF in C major.

Students should first be given experience in recognizing chords that are the same or different, using guitar, autoharp, or piano. A simple song using only two chord changes ("Polly Wolly Doodle," "He's Got the Whole World," "Sandy Land," "Springfield Mountain") may be sung with only the I chord. Students will recognize that this is unpleasant and dull. By asking students to suggest the place of the first chord change, the harmonic pattern may be constructed on the board.

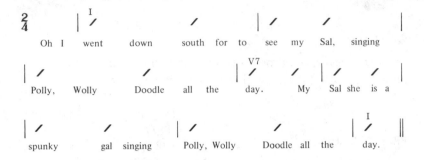

$\frac{2}{4}$ | I / / | / / |

Oh I   went   down   south for to   see my   Sal,   singing

| / / | Doodle all the   V7 /   / | / / |

Polly,   Wolly   Doodle all the   day.   My   Sal she is a

| / / | / / | I / ‖

spunky   gal singing   Polly, Wolly   Doodle all the   day.

This may be done in two keys, demonstrating the constant relationship of the chords. It is also preparatory to transposition.

The students may then be introduced to a song using the three primary chords: I, IV, and V. for example, "Glory, Glory, Hallelujah," early rock tunes, and much folk music.

Through performance of harmonic accompaniments to familiar tunes using tone-bell chords, autoharps, guitars, or by playing the degree of the scale on a melodic percussion instrument, familiarity develops to where students may attempt the final evaluation.

EVALUATION

Students will select appropriate chords for "Happy Birthday" after the I, IV, and V chords are sounded. Given the outline of words and chord slashes, students will suggest places for chord changes and select the I, IV, or V chord for each change.

Teacher's Reference:

$\frac{3}{4}$ 𝄾 | / / / | / / / | / / / | / / / |

        I   V7   I

Happy Birthday to   you   Happy Birthday   to   you   Happy

| / / / | / / / | / / / | / / / ‖

                       IV   I   V7   I

Birth - day   to   - - - - - - - - Happy   Birth - day   to   you.

139

31. HARMONY: TRANSPOSING MELODIES

OBJECTIVE

Students will learn that if a song is too high or too low for a singing range, it may be transposed by choosing a key-note *(do)* higher or lower than the original key-note. Students will also realize that it is possible to find the new set of chords by identifying the relationship of the first set and transferring this relationship to the new key.

PROCEDURES

Transposition is moving a song to a different pitch level while keeping interval relationships the same. Vocalists often transpose to fit songs into a more comfortable range. Instrumentalists sometimes transpose songs into different keys to add interest to otherwise identical repetitions. By using a capo guitarists can transpose songs up while keeping the same fingering patterns. For each fret that the capo is moved up the fingerboard, the key is transposed one half-step higher.

After singing the first phrase of "Kum Ba Yah" in three different keys as given below, ask one student to verbally describe what the differences were. Note that all the internal pitch relationships stayed constant; that is, the song still sounded the same, except that the overall pitch level was higher with each transposition. By starting with the last example and proceeding to the first, the pitch level moves lower.

Chord Relationship:

EVALUATION

1. Students will explain the definition of transposition—moving a piece of music to a different pitch level while keeping all interval relationships constant.

2. Students will explain that, after transposition, the song is the same song, in a different key, starting on a different note, with a different set of chords having the same relationship as the first set of chords.

32. HARMONY: RECOGNIZING HARMONIC RHYTHM

OBJECTIVE

Students will notate the rhythm created by chord changes in a song.

PROCEDURES

Chord changes produce what is called *harmonic rhythm*. Have students write the total time duration of each chord in a song. It may be necessary to use ties if the chord lasts longer than one measure or if it just continues over one measure. For instance, the chorus to "Drunken Sailor" would have the harmonic rhythm notated as follows:

Another way to notate harmonic rhythm is to represent each beat with either a chord symbol or a diagonal line. The diagonal line indicates another beat of the same chord:

$\frac{2}{4}$ ⁄ ⁄ | ⁄ ⁄ | ⁄ ⁄ | ⁄ ⁄ | ⁄ ⁄ | ⁄ ⁄ | ⁄ ⁄ | ⁄ ⁄ ‖
Dm   C   Dm   C   Dm

Harmonic Rhythm:

$\frac{2}{4}$ 𝅗𝅥＿𝅗𝅥 | 𝅗𝅥＿𝅗𝅥 | 𝅗𝅥＿𝅗𝅥 | 𝅗𝅥 | 𝅗𝅥 ‖
Dm   C   Dm   C   Dm

EVALUATION

1. Given tone bells to form the E ♭ (E ♭ –G–B ♭) and the B ♭ ₇ (B ♭ –D–F–A ♭) chords, two groups of students will notate the harmonic rhythm of "Tom Dooley" and accompany the class in singing the song.

2. Students will write the harmonic rhythm of "Oh Susanna" and accompany the class singing the song on the autoharp in the key of C major (transposition key: D = C, G = F, A₇ = G₇).

33. HARMONY: MELODIC TEXTURE

OBJECTIVE

Students will perform and identify textures in musical examples.

PROCEDURES

Texture refers to the way in which simultaneous sounds and melodic lines are combined in a piece of music. The three principal textures may be described simply as (a) music that has a single melody, (b) music that has a melody with an accompaniment, and (c) music that has several melodic lines played or sung simultaneously.

Some people teach the above concepts using words such as *monophonic, homophonic,* and *polyphonic.* The following outline is given as a guide to the teacher who will adapt the information to the three simple categories given above.

Musical texture may be *monophonic* (one sound) or *polyphonic* (more than one sound).

Monophonic texture consists of a single melodic line without harmonic accompaniment. Gregorian chant and some non-Western music make good examples of monophonic texture. Unison singing without accompaniment is also an example of monophonic texture.

Polyphonic texture may be *Homophonic,* where sounds are played together, for example, a hymn tune, or *contrapuntal,* where several distinct melodic lines are heard, for example a round or fugue.

EVALUATION

Students will suggest and perform music which (1) has a single melody line, (2) has a melody with accompaniment, and (3) has several melodic lines played simultaneously.

34. FORM: IDENTIFYING PHRASES

OBJECTIVE

Students will identify phrases in songs.

PROCEDURES

A *musical phrase* is (1) a succession of tones having pitch and duration, (2) a division of the melodic line comparable to a sentence in speech, and (3) often the amount of melody included between breaths taken by a singer. The end of a phrase is called a *cadence*. The cadence tone of a phrase is often a longer durational value than most of the other tones in the phrase. Phrases can end with either a half cadence (a sense of incompleteness) or a full cadence (a sense of completeness).

Students will sing "Yankee Doodle" paying particular attention to the notation of the song and identify phrases and cadences. Stop the song at each cadence and determine if it is a half or a full cadence. Emphasize the musical necessity to continue the melody after a half cadence and the possibility of stopping after a full cadence.

The concepts of phrase length and cadence points are easily illustrated by having students participate in physical movement, for example, directional changes in arm movements and walking, to demonstrate the end of one phrase and the beginning of another by contrasting movements.

EVALUATION

Students will identify the phrases and cadences in "America, the Beautiful" and sing the song, breathing only at cadences.

Can dynamics be used to influence and enhance the musical intent and contour of a phrase?

35. FORM: RECOGNIZING SAME/DIFFERENT PHRASES

OBJECTIVE

Students will identify parts of songs which are the same or different, and will explain what is meant by introduction, transition (bridge), and coda and relate these to a pop song.

PROCEDURES

Form in music refers to design or structure. The study of this increases comprehension and memory. Beginning instruction should stress the parts of melodies which are the same or different and should build upon this to show how differences are created (melody, rhythm, tone color), the effect of these differences, and how the different sections are united.

Take several short well-known melodies with two markedly contrasting sections. The first part of the melody is identified as A and the second as B. The teacher and students will listen to a record or perform a song and write down the succession of A's and B's. Students will be greatly helped if, initially, the teacher isolates the place of the change.

After this is established, introductions (music which precedes the A theme), transitions or bridges (music which links two sections) and codas (music which is added onto the main body of the piece as a conclusion) should be discussed and illustrated.

EVALUATION

Students will outline the form of a current pop tune. It is beneficial to execute this evaluation with the teacher and the group, then with students in small groups, with the final evaluation occurring through individually written outlines. This may be done over several lessons.

An example of a written outline would be

Intro.　A　A　B　Bridge　B　A　B　Coda

36. FORM: UNDERSTANDING STROPHIC FORM

OBJECTIVE

Students will identify songs in which the form consists of the same melody repeated several times to different words.

PROCEDURES

A *melody* is a musically independent unit having (1) tones with pitch and duration, (2) two or more phrases (usually), and (3) a sense of completeness. A *song* is a melody with words performed vocally and (usually) with instrumental accompaniment.

Sometimes musical ideas are expanded into longer pieces by repeating the same musical material to different words (that is, several stanzas of text are sung to the same melody). This type of musical expansion is called *strophic form*. Contrast and variety come from the vocal delivery and accompanimental changes in each presentation of the text.

Sometimes the chorus is sung to the same melody as the verse (as in "Tum Balalaika") and sometimes the chorus is sung to a different melody (as in "Yankee Doodle").

Students will identify phrases and explain how the musical structure expands in "The Fox" and in "Oh Susanna."

EVALUATION

Students will verbalize how the musical form of several selected songs is expanded in strophic form.

37. FORM: VARIATION FORM

OBJECTIVE

Students will define "theme and variations" as a musical form in which a melody is repeated several times, with each repetition being different.

PROCEDURES

Too much repetition in a piece can make it boring, especially if there is not a text to sustain the listener's attention. Discuss the elements of music which a composer can alter to give new interest to repetitions of a melody (tone color, mode, beat tempo, beat subdivision/-grouping, melodic ornaments, harmony, dynamics).

Students will listen to an illustrative song, for example, "The Trout" by Franz Schubert. Phrases and other elements of this song will be identified and students will sing the melody on a neutral syllable. After becoming familiar with the song, students might listen to the Andantino from "The Trout Quintet" by Schubert. Is all of the melody used in the Andantino?

The text and musical notation of songs can be found in basal series. In most cases, recordings and excerpts of orchestral scores are provided. Students can follow the progress of the theme throughout the variations by pointing to the notation of the theme.

EVALUATION

Students will identify and describe the altered elements in each variation. The instrument playing the melody should be identified in each variation.

	Instrument playing melody	Mode	Instrument playing varied element
Theme	Violin	Major	
Variation I	Piano	Major	Cello/Viola/Violin
Variation II	Cello/Viola	Major	Violin
Variation III	Cello/S. Bass	Major	Piano
Variation IV		Minor	Tutti (all)
Variation V	Cello	Major	Piano (Violin interlude)
Variation VI	Violin/Cello	Major	Piano/Violin

38. FORM: RECOGNIZING MUSICAL FORMS

OBJECTIVE

Students will aurally identify at least one of the following forms when presented with a piece of music.

PROCEDURES

Similar to tone color, *form* is an aspect of every piece of music and can be either the central topic of a lesson or merely provide reinforcing information which helps explain the musical intent of a composition. The following outline provides the briefest of surveys of the subject. The two preceding lessons may be used as models for developing further lessons with other musical forms. Many multi-movement forms are quite common. Multi-movement vocal forms include the Mass, cantata, oratorio, passion, and opera. Multi-movement instrumental forms include the sonata, concerto, concerto grosso, symphony, and suite. The length of such works usually precludes presenting them for a typical music lesson; however, single movements or sections of these larger works may be used effectively.

Music which contains a text often takes its form from the text itself, the words providing the direction of expansion for the music. However, if no text is involved, the composer must design his piece through the combination of abstract musical ideas. One example of expanding a piece of music through such a technique is variation form, in which a musical idea is repeated several times with some aspect of the music altered on each repetition. Other examples of musical forms are given below.

Excellent materials for teaching lessons on form can be found in *Adventures in Music* and its accompanying manuals and recordings. Materials for lessons on form from basal series texts, music history and literature texts, and some record jackets are easily obtained.

SINGLE MOVEMENT FORMS

A B   This form has two contrasting sections. The song "America" may be conceived as a small AB form. The A section includes the words "My Country, 'tis of Thee, sweet land of liberty, of Thee I sing." The B section includes the remainder of the first verse of text.

ABA   This is the most popular musical form. It is sometimes called song form or ternary form. "Twinkle, Twinkle Little Star" is an example of a very small ABA form. The words "like a diamond in the sky, up above the world so high" comprise the B section.

Song   A short composition for voice, usually accompanied and based on a poetic text. A song may be strophic or through-composed and is usually in binary (AB) or ternary (ABA) form.

Theme and Variations   A form in which a musical idea (usually the melody) is changed with each repetition of the idea.

Rondo   A musical form in which the opening section (A) returns after contrasting sections have been introduced. A typical rondo form is ABACA.

Sonata Form   A form consisting of an exposition of one or two themes, a development of those themes, and a recapitulation of the original statement of the themes. An introduction and/or a coda may be included to further expand this form.

Fugue   A form consisting of the exposition of a musical subject in polyphonic texture. That is, one main theme is treated in imitative style like a round. Sections called episodes contrast with statements of the subject.

Free Form   No standard or regular structures are employed in the piece. The symphonic poem is an example. In a symphonic poem the music's structural progress is determined by an extra-musical idea or story.

EVALUATION

Students will listen to a piece of music, outline the form, and relate this outline to one of the musical forms listed.

39. SYNTHESIS: ANALYZING MUSIC BY COMPARISONS

OBJECTIVE

Students will compare the musical qualities of two short (1 to 2 minutes) pieces of music.

PROCEDURES

To assist the students' comparison of two pieces of music, an outline appropriate for the age level should be prepared. Students should be encouraged to add objective and subjective comments.

EVALUATION

Students will listen to two contrasting pieces of music in the same genre (for example, concert, folk, pop) and list musical qualities which describe each.

DYNAMICS	loud soft	
MOOD	lively calm	
METER	steady not steady moves in 2 or 3	
RHYTHM	smooth bouncy	
STEADY BEAT	yes no sometimes	
MELODY	easy/difficult to sing moves in skips/steps	
HARMONY	many/few chord changes	
TEMPO	fast faster slow slower	
VOICES	yes no what kind?	
INSTRUMENTS	percussion	
	brass	
	strings	
	woodwinds	
COMMENTS		

Other illustrations of variation form include Mozart—"Variations" on "Ah, vous dirai-je, Maman," Calliet—"Variations on Pop! Goes the Weasel," and Ives—"Variations on America."

40. SYNTHESIS: CONDUCTING

OBJECTIVE

Students will conduct songs with beat groupings of 2, 3, and 4, that is, in 2, 3, and 4 meter.

PROCEDURES

The conductor of a band, chorus, or orchestra is responsible for (1) getting the group started and stopped properly, (2) determining the tempo, (3) maintaining the beat, (4) indicating tempo changes, and (5) suggesting dynamics, phrasing, and other expressive qualities.

Conductors usually follow patterns which correspond to the beat groupings per measure. The first beat in beat grouping patterns is always down in a central body position. Three common conducting patterns used by conductors are given as follows:

Beat Groupings of 2   Beat Groupings of 3   Beat Groupings of 4

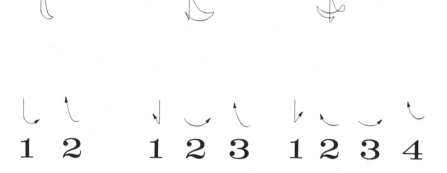

Students who chose to conduct with the left hand will reverse these patterns.

Before attempting to conduct these patterns, students should be reminded to listen for the first beat of the group in each musical example. This may be indicated by a clap or by showing the down-beat in the conducting pattern.

For clarity, in beginning a group together, the conductor gives a preparatory beat which is the indication in the pattern for the beat which immediately precedes the starting beat of the music.

Conducting is most effectively learned by working with "live" performances.

EVALUATION

Individual students will conduct the class in selected songs.

THREE
SELECTED RESOURCE GUIDE

References

SPECIFIC AREA OF REFERENCE

BOOKS FOR CHILDREN

Balet, Jan. *What Makes an Orchestra?* New York: Oxford University Press, 1951.

Britten, Benjamin, and Imogene Holst. *The Wonderful World of Music.* New York: Garden City Books, 1958.

Buchanan, Fannie, and Charles Luckenbill. *How Man Made Music.* Chicago, Ill.: Follett Publishing Co., 1959.

Bunche, Jane. *Introduction to the Instruments of the Orchestra.* New York: Golden Press, 1962.

Davis, Lionel, and Edith Davis. *Keyboard Instruments.* Minnesota: Lerner Publications Co., 1963.

Edgerly, Beatrice. *From the Hunter's Blow.* New York: G. P. Putnam's Sons, 1942.

Emberly, Ed, and Barbara Emberly. *Drummer Hoff.* Englewood Cliffs, N.J.: Prentice-Hall Inc., 1967.

Frost, Bruno. *A Child's Book of Music Makers.* Chicago, Ill.: Maxton Publishing Co., 1957.

Geralton, James. *The Story of Sound.* New York: Harcourt Brace Jovanovich, 1948.

Gilmore, Lee. *Folk Instruments.* Minnesota: Lerner Publications Co., 1962.

Huntington, Harriet E. *Tune Up.* New York: Doubleday and Co., 1942.

Kettelkamp, Larry. *Drums, Rattles, and Bells; Flutes, Whistles, and Reeds; Singing Strings.* New York: William Morrow and Co., 1960.

Kinscella, Hanzel G. Readers in Music Appreciation:
Book 4   *Folk Tales from Many Lands* (1959)
Book 5   *Conrad's Magic Flight* (1959)
Book 6   *Tales of Olden Days* (1960)
Book 7   *Around the World in Story* (1952)
Book 8   *History Sings* (1957)
Lincoln, Neb.: University Publishing Co.

Lacey, Marion. *Picture Book of Musical Instruments.* New York: Lothrop, Lee, and Shephard Co., 1952.

Marquis, Margaret H. *Rhythms, Rhymes and Songs for Rhythm and Melody Instruments.* New York: Holnew Publications, 1965.

Posell, Elsa Z. *This Is an Orchestra.* Boston, Mass.: Houghton Mifflin Co., 1950.

Richardson, A. L. *Tooters, Tweeters, Strings and Beaters.* New York: Grossett & Dunlap, Inc., 1964.

Suggs, William. *Meet the Orchestra.* New York: The Macmillan Co., 1966.

Warren, F., and Lee Warren. *The Music of Africa.* Englewood Cliffs, N.J.: Prentice-Hall, Inc., 1970.

CARABO-CONE

Books

Carabo-Cone, Madeleine. *How to Help Children Learn Music.* New York: Harper & Row Publishers, 1955.

Carabo-Cone, Madeleine. *The Playground as Music Teacher.* New York: Harper & Row Publishers, 1959.

Articles

Carabo-Cone, Madeleine. "Learning How to Learn: A Sensory Motor Approach." *Music Journal,* 37(1), 1973, p. 16.

CREATIVITY

Books

Andrews, Gladys. *Creative Rhythmic Movement for Children.* Englewood Cliffs, N.J.: Prentice-Hall, Inc., 1954.

Cheyette, Irving, and Herbert Cheyette. *Teaching Music Creatively in the Elementary School.* New York: McGraw-Hill Book Co., 1969.

Contemporary Music Project. *Experiments in Musical Creativity.* Washington, D.C.: Music Educators National Conference, 1966.

Coleman, Satis. *Creative Music in the Home.* Valparaiso, Indiana: Myers, 1928.

Experiments in Musical Creativity. Contemporary Music Project for Creativity, Washington, D.C.: MENC, 1965.

Hickok, Dorothy, and James A. Smith. *Creative Teaching of Music in the Elementary School.* Boston, Mass.: Allyn and Bacon, Inc., 1974.

Luck, James T. *Creative Music for the Classroom Teacher.* New York: Random House, 1971.

Marsh, Mary Val. *Explore and Discover Music: Creative Approaches to Music in Elementary, Middle and Junior High School.* London: Macmillan Co., 1970.

Nielsen, Floraine, and Roger Folstrom. *Music Fundamentals: A Creative Activities Approach.* Reading, Mass.: Addison-Wesley Publishing Co., 1969.

Rosenberg, Martha. *It's Fun to Teach Creative Music.* New York: The Play Schools Association, 1963.

Saffran, Rosana B. *First Book of Creative Rhythms.* New York: Holt, Rinehart and Winston, Inc., 1963.

Snyder, Alice. *Creating Music with Children.* New York: Music Mills, 1957.

Thackray, Rupert Manfred. *Creative Music in Education.* London: Novella, 1966.

Articles

Aronoff, Frances Webber. "Involving the Young Child in Music: Games Teachers Play." *Music Educators Journal, 57*(6), 1971, p. 27.

Boardman, Eunice. "New Sounds in the Classroom." *Music Educators Journal, 55*(3), 1968, p. 62.

Hoenack, Peg. "Unleash Creativity—Let Them Improvise!" *Music Educators Journal, 57*(9), 1971, p. 33.

Holderried, Elizabeth Swist. "Creativity in My Classroom." *Music Educators Journal, 55*(7), 1969, p. 37.

Jensen, Eric. "Creativity and Its Sources." *Music Educators Journal, 55*(7), 1969, p. 34.

Landis, Beth. "Experiments in Creativity." *Music Educators Journal, 54*(9), 1968, p. 41.

DALCROZE

Books

Dalcroze, Emile Jacques. *The Eurhythmics of Jacques Dalcroze.* London: Constable and Co., Ltd., 1972.

Dalcroze, Emile Jacques. *Rhythm, Music and Education.* New York: G. P. Putnam, 1921.

Driver, Ethel. *A Pathway to Dalcroze Eurhythmics.* New York: Thomas Nelson, 1951.

Findlay, Elsa. *Rhythm and Movement—Application of Dalcroze Eurhythmics.* Evanston, Ill.: Summy-Birchard Co., 1971.

Gell, Heather. *Music, Movement and the Young Child.* Sydney, Australia: Australasian Publishing Co., 1969.

Landis, Beth, and Polly Carter. *Eclectic Curriculum in American Music Education: Contributions of Dalcroze, Kodaly, Orff.* Washington, D.C.: MENC, 1972.

Rosentrauch, Henrietta. *Percussion, Rhythm, Music, Movement.* Pittsburgh, Pa.: Volkwein Bros., 1970.

Articles

Willow, Judith. "Beginning with Delight, Leading to Wisdom: Dalcroze." *Music Educators Journal, 56*(1), 1969, p. 72.

KODALY

Books

Choksy, Lois. *The Kodaly Method: Comprehensive Music Education from Infant to Adult.* Englewood Cliffs, N.J.: Prentice-Hall, Inc., 1974.

Eosze, Laszlo. *Zoltan Kodaly: His Life and Work.* Boston, Mass.: Crescendo Publishing Co., 1962.

Kodaly, Zoltan. *Let Us Sing Correctly.* New York: Boosey and Hawkes, 1952.

Major New Movements in Elementary School Music Education: Suzuki, Kodaly, Orff. Albany, New York: State Education Department, Bureau of Music Education, 1969.

Szabo, Helga. *The Kodaly Concept of Music Education.* New York: Boosey & Hawkes, 1968.

Wheeler, Lawrence, and Lois Raebeck. *Orff and Kodaly Adapted for the Elementary School.* Dubuque, Iowa: Wm. C. Brown Co. Publisher, 1972.

Articles

Bacon, Denise. "Kodaly and Orff: Report from Europe." *Music Educators Journal, 55*(8), 1969, p. 53.

Edwards, Loraine. "The Great Animating Stream of Music." *Music Educators Journal, 57*(6), 1971, p. 38.

Kokas, Klara. "Kodaly's Concept in Children's Education." *Music Journal, 29*(7), 1971, p. 27.

MANHATTANVILLE

Books

Biasini, Americole, Ronald Thomas, and Lenore Pogonowski. *MMCP Interaction.* 2nd edition. Bardonia, New York: Media Materials.

Thomas, Ronald. *MMCP Synthesis.* Bardonia, New York: Media Materials.

Articles

Harvey, Arthur W. "A Conductor in Every Chair." *Music Educators Journal, 58*(6), 1972, p. 46.

Messicks, Lillian V. "Make Room for the Different Drummer." *Music Educators Journal, 58*(2), 1971, p. 23.

Thomas, Ronald B. "Innovative Music Education Programs." *Music Educators Journal, 53*(9), 1967, p. 50.

Thomas, Ronald B. "Rethinking the Curriculum." *Music Educators Journal,* 56(6), 1970, p. 68.

MONTESSORI

Books

Macheroni, Anna Maria. *Developing the Musical Senses: The Montessori Approach to Music for the Ear, Voice, Eye, and Hand.* Cincinnati, Ohio: Greenwood Press, 1967.

Montessori, Maria. *Dr. Montessori's Own Handbook.* New York: Schocken Books, 1965. Original 1914.

Montessori, Maria. *The Montessori Method.* New York: Schocken Books, 1964.

ORFF

Books

Landis, Beth, and Polly Carter. *The Eclectic Curriculum in American Music Education: Contributions of Dalcroze, Kodaly and Orff.* Washington, D.C.: MENC, 1972.

Nichols, Elizabeth. *Orff Instrument Source Book.* Morristown, N.J.: Silver Burdett Co., 1970. Volumes I, II.

Wheeler, Lawrence, and Lois Raebeck. *Orff and Kodaly Adapted for the Elementary School,* 2nd ed. Dubuque, Iowa: Wm. C. Brown Co. Publisher, 1972.

Articles

Bacon, Denise. "Kodaly and Orff: Report from Europe." *Music Educators Journal,* 55(8), 1969, p. 53.

Bevans, Judith. "The Exceptional Child and Orff." *Music Educators Journal,* 55(7), 1969, p. 40.

Flagg, Marion. "The Orff System in Today's World." *Music Educators Journal,* 53(4), 1966, p. 30.

Frazee, Jane C. "The Mystery of the Orffs." *Music Educators Journal,* 55(2), 1968, p. 64.

Mittleman, Lois Rosenblum. "Orff and the Urban Child." *Music Educators Journal,* 55(7), 1969, p. 40.

Nichols, Elizabeth L. "Orff Can Work in Every Classroom." *Music Educators Journal,* 57(1), 1970, p. 43.

Wonson, Mary L. "Teaching Music with Instant Results: The Creative Orff Approach." *Musart,* 25(2), 1973, p. 42.

SUZUKI

Books

Cook, Clifford A. *Suzuki Education in Action,* 1st ed. New York: Exposition Press, 1970.

Suzuki, Shin'ichi. *Nurtured by Love: A new Approach to Education.* New York: Exposition Press, 1969.

Articles

Brunson, Theodore R. "A Visit with Dr. Suzuki." *Music Educators Journal,* 55(9), 1969, p. 54.

"Faces of Suzuki." *Music Educators Journal,* 58(7), 1972, p. 54.

Garson, Alfred. "Learning with Suzuki." *Music Educators Journal,* 56(6), 1970, p. 64.

Garson, Alfred. "Suzuki and Physical Movement." *Music Educators Journal,* 60(4), 1973, p. 34.

Kendall, John. "Talent Education and Suzuki." *Music Educators National Conference,* 1966, p. 6.

Roche, M. "How to Lead Your Child to Music." *House and Garden* *126*, 1964, p. 182.

Smith, Herbert. "Some Conclusions Concerning the Suzuki Method of Teaching Violin." *American String Teacher, 15,* 1965, p. 1.

WORLD CULTURES

Books

Malm, William P. *Music Cultures of the Pacific, the Near East and Asia.* Englewood Cliffs, N.J.: Prentice-Hall, 1966.

Nettl, Bruno. *Folk and Traditional Music of the Western Continents.* Englewood Cliffs, N.J.: Prentice-Hall, 1965.

Powers, William K. *Here Is Your Hobby: India Dancing and Costumes.* New York: G. P. Putnam, 1966.

Reeder, Barbara, and James A. Standifer. *A Source Book of Afro-American Materials for Music Educators.* Washington, D.C.: MENC, Contemporary Music Project, 1972.

Sandor, Frigyes, ed. *Music Education in Hungary.* London: Barrie and Rockcliff, 1966.

Southern, Eileen. *The Music of Black Americans: A History.* New York: W. W. Norton & Co., 1971.

Articles

Ballard, Louis W. "Put American Indian Music in the Classroom." *Music Educators Journal, 56*(7), 1970, p. 38.

Curtiss, Marie Joy. "India." *Music Educators Journal, 56*(1), 1969, p. 60.

Edwards, Walford I. "Africa." *Music Educators Journal, 56*(1), 1969, p. 63.

Gillett, Dorothy K. "Hawaiian Music for Hawaii's Children." *Music Educators Journal, 59*(2), 1972, p. 73.

Gaines, Leonard. "Musics of Africa South of the Sahara." *Music Educators Journal, 59*(2), 1972, p. 46.

Grame, Theodore C. "Musics of European Folk Traditions." *Music Educators Journal, 59*(2), 1972, p. 52.

McAllester, David P. "Musics of the Americas." *Music Educators Journal, 59*(92), 1972, p. 54.

MENC. "Music in World Cultures." *Music Educators Journal, 59*(2), 1972, p. 126.

Menon, Narayana. "Musics of South Asia." *Music Educators Journal, 59*(2), 1972, p. 40.

Nketia, J. H. Kwabena. "Music Education in Africa and the West: We Can Learn from Each Other." *Music Educators Journal, 57*(3), 1970, p. 48

Reeder, Barbara. "Afro Music: As Tough as a Mozart Quartet." *Music Educators Journal, 56*(5), 1970, p. 88.

Slobin, Mark. "Musics of West Asia." *Music Educators Journal, 59* (2), 1972, p. 44.

Standifer, James A. "Listening Is an Equal Opportunity Art." *Music Educators Journal, 56*(5), 1970, p. 97.

Susilo, Hardja. "Musics of Southeast Asia." *Music Educators Journal, 59*(2), 1972, p. 35.

Yamaguchi, Osamu. "Musics of Northeast Asia." *Music Educators Journal, 59*(2), 1972, p. 30.

YOUTH MUSIC

Articles

Elliott, Dorothy Gail. "Junk Music." *Music Educators Journal, 58*(5), 1972, p. 58.

Fowler, Charles B. "The Case Against Rock: A Reply." *Music Educators Journal, 57*(1), 1970, p. 38.

Fox, Sidney. "From Rock to Bach." *Music Educators Journal, 56* (9), 1970, p. 52.

Helm, Sanford M. "Jazz: Music History in Miniature." *Music Educators Journal, 51*(4), 1965, p. 53.

MacCluskey, Thomas. "Rock in Its Elements." *Music Educators Journal, 56*(3), 1969, p. 4.

Willis, Thomas. "Youth Music on Their Terms." *Music Educators Journal, 56*(9), 1970, p. 56.

"Youth Music: A Special Report." *Music Educators Journal, 56*(3), 1969, p. 43.

GENERAL REFERENCES

GENERAL MUSIC BOOKS

Books

Abramson, Robert M. *Rhythm Games.* New York: Music and Movement Press, 1973.

Adam, Jeno. *Growing in Music With Movable Do.* New York: Pannonius Central Service, Inc., 1971.

Addison, Richard. *Begin Making Music, Make Music, Make More Music.* Scotland: Holmes McDougall Ltd., 1967.

Andrew, Frances, and Clara Cockerile. *Your School Music Program.* Englewood Cliffs, N.J.: Prentice-Hall, Inc., 1958.

Andrews, Jay A., and Jeanne F. Wardian. *Introduction to Music Fundamentals: A Program Text for Elementary Education,* 3rd ed. New York: Appleton-Century-Crofts, 1972.

Aronoff, Fran. *Music for Young Children.* New York: Holt, Rinehart and Winston, 1969.

Austin, Virginia. *Learning Fundamental Concepts of Music: An Activities Approach.* Dubuque, Iowa: Wm. C. Brown Co., Publishers, 1970.

Bacon, Ernst. *Words of Music.* Syracuse, New York: Syracuse University Press, 1960.

Baird, Peggy F. *Music Books for the Elementary School Library.* Washington, D.C.: MENC, 1972.

Baldwin, Lillian Luverne. *A Listener's Anthology of Music.* New York: Silver Burdett, 1948.

Baldwin, Lillian Luverne. *Music for Young Listeners.* New York: Silver Burdett, 1951. 3 vols.

Baldwin, Lillian Luverne. *Music to Remember: A Book for Listeners.* New York: Silver Burdett, 1951.

Batcheller, John M., and Sally Monsour. *Music in Recreation and Leisure.* Dubuque, Iowa: Wm. C. Brown Co. Publishers, 1972.

Beer, Alice S., and Mary E. Hoffman. *Teaching Music: What, How, Why.* Morristown, N.J.: General Learning Press, 1973.

Bergethon, Bjornar, and Eunice Boardman. *Musical Growth in the Elementary School,* 3rd ed. New York: Holt, Rinehart and Winston, 1975.

Berning, Alice B. *Keyboard Experiences for Classroom Teachers.* Dubuque, Iowa: Wm. C. Brown Co. Publishers, 1976.

Bernstein, Leonard. *Young People's Concerts.* New York: Simon and Schuster, 1970.

Birge, Edward B. *History of Public School Music in the United States.* New York: Oliver Ditson, 1938.

Brian, Dennis. *Experimental Music in Schools: Towards a New World of Sound.* London: Oxford University Press Music Dept., 1970.

Brooks, B. Marion. *Music Education in the Elementary School.* New York: American Book Company, 1946.

Burakoff, Gerald, and Wheeler Lawrence. *Music Making in the Elementary School.* New York: Hargail Music, Inc.

Cheyette, Irving, and Herbert Cheyette. *Teaching Music Creatively in The Elementary School.* New York: McGraw-Hill Book Co., 1969.

Children and Music. Washington, D.C.: Association for Childhood Education (International), 1948.

Clegg, Alec. *Revolution in the British Primary Schools.* Washington, D.C.: National Association of Elementary School Principals, 1971.

Clough, John. *Scales, Intervals, Keys, and Triads: A Self-Instruction Program.* New York: W.W. Norton, 1964.

Coleman, Satis Narrona. *The Book of Bells.* New York: The John Day Co., 1938.

Colwell, Richard. *The Evaluation of Music Teaching and Learning.* Englewood Cliffs. N.J.: Prentice-Hall, Inc., 1970.

Colwell, Richard. *The Teaching of Instrumental Music.* New York: Meredith Corp., 1969.

Cope, David. *New Directions in Music.* Dubuque, Iowa: Wm. C. Brown Co., Publishers, 1971.

Darazs, Arpad, and Stephen Jay. *Sight and Sound.* Oceanside, New York: Boosey and Hawkes, Inc., 1965.

Dobbs, Jack P. *The Slow Learner and Music: A Handbook for Teachers.* New York: Oxford University Press, 1966.

Doll, Edna, and Mary J. Nelson. *Rhythms Today.* Morristown, N.J.: Silver Burdett Co., 1965.

Driver, Ann. *Music and Movement.* New York: Oxford University Press, 1966.

Dykema, Peter, and Hannah Gundiff. *School Music Handbook.* Boston, Mass.: C. C. Birchard, 1939.

Elementary Science Study. *The Musical Instrument Recipe Book.* New York: McGraw-Hill, 1971.

Eliott, Raymond. *Learning and Teaching Music.* Columbus, Ohio: Charles E. Merrill Books, Inc., 1966.

Ellison, Alfred. *Music with Children.* New York: McGraw-Hill, 1959.

Ernst, Karl D., and Charles L. Gary (ed.). *Music in General Education.* Washington, D.C.: Music Educators National Conference, 1965.

Farnsworth, Paul R. *The Social Psychology of Music.* New York: Dryden Press, 1958.

Faulhaber, Martha, and John Hawkinson. *Rhythms, Music, and Instruments to Make.* Chicago, Ill.: Albert Whitmas, 1970.

Flannigan, Marguerite Nigro. *Free and Inexpensive Teaching Aids for Music Education.* Wankepan, Ill.: Teaching Aids Library, 1964.

Fleming, William. *Art, Music and Ideas.* New York: Holt, Rinehart and Winston, 1970.

Garretson, Robert. *Music in Childhood Education,* 2nd ed. New York: Appleton-Century-Crofts, 1976.

Gary, Charles L. *The Study of Music in the Elementary School: A Conceptual Approach.* Washington D.C.: MENC, 1967.

Gelineau, Phyllis R. *Experiences in Music,* 2nd ed. New York: McGraw-Hill Book Co., 1976.

Gell, Heather. *Music, Movement and the Young Child.* Australasian Publishing Co.; Available Volkwein Bros., Pittsburgh, Pa., 1969.

Geri, Frank. *Illustrated Games and Rhythms for Children.* Englewood Cliffs, N.J.: Prentice-Hall, Inc., 1955.

Gordon, Edwin. *The Psychology of Music Teaching.* Englewood Cliffs, N.J.: Prentice-Hall, Inc., 1971.

Grant, Parks. *Music for Elementary Teachers,* 2nd ed. New York: Appleton-Century-Crofts, 1960.

Green, Elizabeth. *Orchestral Bowings and Routines.* Ann Arbor, Michigan: Ann Arbor Publishers, 1957.

Green, Elizabeth. *Teaching Stringed Instruments in Classes.* Englewood Cliffs, N.J.: Prentice-Hall, Inc., 1966.

Greenberg, Marvin, and Beatrix MacGregor. *Music Handbook for the Elementary School.* New York: Parker Publishing Co., 1972.

Hall, Doreen, and Arnold Walter. *Music for Children.* Volumes I-IV. New York: Associated Music Publishers, 1969.

Hargiss, Genevieve. *Music for Elementary Teachers: A Programmed Course in Basic Theory and Keyboard Chording.* New York: Appleton-Century-Crofts, 1968.

Hartsell, O. M. *Teaching Music in the Elementary School—Opinion and Comment.* Washington, D. C.: Association for Supervision and Curriculum Development, MENC, 1964.

Henry, Nelson (ed.). *Basic Concepts in Music Education.* Chicago, Ill.: National Society for the Study of Education, Fifty-seventh yearbook, 1958.

Hermann, Edward J. *Supervising Music in the Elementary School.* Englewood Cliffs, N.J.: Prentice-Hall, Inc., 1965.

Hickok, Dorothy, and James A. Smith. *Creative Teaching of Music in the Elementary School.* Boston: Allyn and Bacon, Inc., 1974.

Hood, Marguerite V. *Teaching Rhythm and Classroom Instruments.* Englewood Cliffs, N.J.: Prentice-Hall, Inc., 1966.

Horton, John. *Music, Informal Schools in Britain Today Series.* New York: Citation Press, 1972.

Hughes, William O. *A Concise Introduction to Teaching Elementary School Music.* Belmont, Cal.: Wadsworth Publishing Co., 1973.

Hughes, William O. *Comprehensive Musicianship for Classroom Music.* Reading, Mass.: Addison-Wesley, 1974.

Hughes, William O. and Lee Kjelson. *General Music: A Comprehensive Approach.* Reading, Mass: Addison-Wesley, 1975.

Humphreys, M. Lois, and J. Ross. *Interpreting Music Through Movement.* Englewood Cliffs, N.J.: Prentice-Hall, Inc., 1964.

Hunter, Hilda. *Growing Up With Music.* Old Tappan, N.J.: Hewitt House, 1970.

Hurd, Lyman C., and Edith Savage. *First Experiences in Music.* Belmont, Cal.: Wadsworth Publishing Co., 1975.

Jacobs, Norman. *Foundations and Frontiers in Music Education.* New York: Holt, Rinehart and Winston, 1966.

Janson, H. W., and Joseph Kerman. *A History of Art and Music.* Englewood Cliffs, N.J.: Prentice-Hall, and New York: Abrams, 1969.

Jones, Archie L. (ed.). *Music Education in Action.* Boston, Mass.: Allyn and Bacon, 1964.

Jones, Genevieve. *Seeds of Movement.* Pittsburgh, Pa.: Volkwein Press, Inc., 1972.

Kaplan, Max. *Foundations and Frontiers of Music Education.* New York: Holt, Rinehart and Winston, 1966.

Kaplan, Max, and Frances J. Steiner. *Musicianship for the Classroom Teacher.* Chicago, Ill.: Rand McNally, 1966.

Kinscella, Haze, and Elizabeth M. Tierney. *The Child and His Music.* Lincoln, Nebraska: University Publishing Co., 1952.

Knuth, Alice, and William Knuth. *Basic Resources for Learning Music.* Belmont, Cal.: Wadsworth Publishing Co., 1966.

Kohut, D. I. *Instrumental Music Pedagogy.* Englewood Cliffs, N.J.: Prentice-Hall, Inc., 1973.

Kowall, Bonnie C. (ed.). *Perspectives in Music Education: Source Book III.* Washington, D.C.: Music Educators National Conference, 1966.

Krone, Beatrice, and Max Krone. *Music Participation in the Elementary School.* Chicago, Ill.: Neil A. Kjos Music Co., 1952.

Labuta, Joseph A., *Guide to Accountability in Music Education.* West Nyack, N.Y.: Parker Publishing Company, Inc., 1974.

Lament, Marylee McMurray. *Music in Elementary Education.* New York: Macmillan Publishing Co., Inc., 1976.

Land, Lois Rhae, and Mary Ann Vaughn. *Music in Today's Classroom: Creating, Listening, Performing.* New York: Harcourt Brace Jovanovich, Inc., 1973.

London, Joseph W. *Leadership for Learning in Music Education.* Costa Mesa, Cal.: Educational Media Press, 1976.

Landeck, Beatrice. *Children and Music: An Informal Guide for Parents and Teachers.* New York: Sloane, 1952.

Landis, Beth, and Polly Carder. *The Eclectic Curriculum in American Music Education: Contributions of Dalcroze, Kodaly, and Orff.* Washington D.C.: Music Educators National Conference, 1972.

Langer, Susanne K. *Feeling and Form: A Theory of Art.* New York: Charles Scribner's Sons, 1953.

Langer, Susanne K. *Philosophy in a New Key,* 3rd ed. New York: New American Library of World Literature, 1957.

Lehman, P. R. *Tests and Measurements in Music.* Englewood Cliffs, N.J.: Prentice-Hall, Inc., 1968.

Leonhard, Charles, and Robert W. House. Revised ed. *Foundations and Principles of Music Education.* New York: McGraw-Hill Co., 1972.

Levin, Gail M., Herbert D. Levin, and Nancy D. Safer. *Learning through Music.* Boston: Teaching Resources Corporation, 1976.

Lewis, Aden. *Listen, Look and Sing.* Morristown, N.J.: Silver Burdett Co., 1971.

Lundin, Robert W., 2nd ed. *An Objective Psychology of Music.* New York: Ronald Press, 1967.

Machlis, Joseph. *The Enjoyment of Music,* 3rd ed. New York: Norton, 1970.

Mandell, Muriel, and Robert E. Wood. *Make Your Own Musical Instruments.* New York: Sterling Publishing Co., Inc., 1957.

Manoff, Tom. *The Music Kit.* New York: W. W. Norton, 1976.

Marsh, Mary V. *Explore and Discover Music,* 2nd ed. New York: The Macmillan Company, 1972.

Matthew, Paul W. *You Can Teach Music, A Handbook for the Classroom Teacher.* New York: Dutton, 1960.

McMillan, L. Eileen. *Guiding Children's Growth Through Music.* Boston: Ginn, 1959.

Meyer, Leonard B. *Emotion and Meaning in Music.* Chicago, Ill.: University of Chicago Press, 1956.

Monsour, Sally, Marilyn Cohan, and Patricia Lindell. *Rhythm in Music and Dance for Children.* Belmont, Cal.: Wadsworth Publishing Co., 1966.

Morgan, Hazel N. (ed.). *Music in American Education: Source Book II.* Washington, D.C.: Music Educators National Conference, 1955.

Morgan, Hazel N. *Music in the Elementary School.* Chicago, Ill.: MENC, 1951.

Motycka, Arthur (ed.) *Music Education for Tomorrow's Society: Selected Topics.* Jamestown, R.I., GAMT Music Press, 1976.

Mursell, James. *Music and the Classroom Teacher.* Morristown, N.J.: Silver Burdett, 1951.

Mursell, James L. *Music Education: Principles and Programs.* Morristown, N.J.: Silver Burdett, 1956.

Mursell, James L. *The Psychology of Music.* New York: W. W. Norton, 1937.

Muscogee Music Project, ESEA Title III, 1972.

Music Education for Elementary School Children. Washington, D.C.: MENC, 1960.

Music Educators' National Conference. *The Study of Music in the Elementary School—A Conceptual Approach.* Washington, D.C.: MENC, 1967.

Music for Children's Living. Washington, D.C.: Association for Childhood Education (International), 1955.

Music in Everyday Living and Learning. Washington, D.C.: MENC, 1960.

Music, K-6, Experimental Edition. Albany, New York: University of the State of New York, State Education Department, Bureau of Curriculum Development, 1972.

Myers, Louise K. *Teaching Children Music in the Elementary School.* Englewood Cliffs, N.J.: Prentice-Hall, Inc., 1961.

Nash, Grace. *Creative Approaches to Child Development with Music, Language and Movement.* New York: Alfred Publishing Co., Inc., 1974.

Nash, Grace. *Today with Music.* New York: Alfred Publishing Co., Inc., 1974.

National Education Association. *Music and Art in the Public Schools.* Research Monograph 1963–M3. Washington, D.C.: National Education Association, 1963.

Nielsen, Floraine, and Roger J. Folstrom. *Music Fundamentals: A Creative Activities Approach.* Reading, Mass.: Addison-Wesley Publishing Company, 1969.

Nordholm, Harriet. *Singing in the Elementary Schools.* Englewood Cliffs, N.J.: Prentice-Hall, Inc., 1966.

Nordoff, Paul, and Clive Robbins. *Therapy in Music for Handicapped Children.* New York: St. Martin's Press, 1972.

Nye, R., N. Aubin, and G. Kyme. *Singing with Children.* Belmont, Cal.: Wadsworth Publishing Co., 1962.

Nye, Robert Evans, and Bjornar Bergethon. *Basic Music, An Activities Approach to Functional Musicianship.* Englewood Cliffs, N.J.: Prentice-Hall, Inc., 1968.

Nye, Robert E., and Bjornar Bergethon. *Basic Music for Classroom Teachers.* Englewood Cliffs, N.J.: Prentice-Hall, Inc., 1962.

Nye, Robert E., and Vernice T. Nye. *Exploring Music with Children.* Belmont, Cal.: Wadsworth Publishing Co., 1966.

Nye, Robert E., and Vernice T. Nye. *Music in the Elementary School,* 4th ed. Englewood Cliffs, N.J.: Prentice-Hall, Inc., 1977.

Nye, Robert E., Vernice T. Nye, and Virginia H. Nye. *Toward World Understanding with Song.* Belmont, Cal.: Wadsworth Publishing Co., 1967.

Nye, Vernice. *Music for Young Children.* Dubuque, Iowa: Wm. C. Brown Co. Publishers, 1975.

Pace, Robert. *Music Essentials for Classroom Teachers.* Belmont, Cal.: Wadworth Publishing Co., 1961.

Pace, Robert. *Piano for Classroom Music.* Englewood Cliffs, N.J.: Prentice-Hall, Inc., 1970.

Pape, Mary. *Growing Up with Music.* London: Oxford University Press, 1970.

Paynter, John. *Hear and Now.* London: Universal Edition, 1972.

Paynter, John, and Peter Aston. *Sound and Silence.* Cambridge, England: University Press, 1970.

Petzold, Robert G. *Auditory Perception of Musical Sounds by Children in the First Six Grades.* Washington, D.C.: HEW Contract, 1966.

Pierce, Anne E. *Teaching Music in the Elementary School.* New York· Holt, Rinehart and Winston, 1959.

Pierce, Anne E., and Neal E. Glenn. *Musicianship for the Elementary Teacher, Theory and Skills Through Songs.* New York: McGraw-Hill Book Co., 1967.

Pound, Gomer. *Music Fundamentals for Teachers.* Dubuque, Iowa: Wm. C. Brown Co. Publishers, 1972.

Puopolo, Vito. *Music Fundamentals.* New York: Schirmer Books, 1976.

Raebeck, Lois, and Lawrence Wheeler. *New Approaches to Music in the Elementary School,* 3rd ed. Dubuque, Iowa: Wm. C. Brown Co. Publishers, 1974.

Regelski, Thomas A. *Principles and Problems of Music Education.* Englewood Cliff, N.J.: Prentice-Hall, Inc., 1975.

Reimer, Bennett. *A Philosophy of Music Education.* Englewood Cliffs, N.J.: Prentice-Hall, Inc., 1970.

Rhoden, Jane Otwell. *A History of Music Written for Pre-School Children.* Tallahassee, Fla.: Unpublished doctoral dissertation, Florida State University, 1969.

Richards, Mary Helen. *Threshold to Music.* San Francisco, Cal.: Fearon Publishers, 1964.

Rinderer, Leo. *Music Education, A Handbook for Music Teaching in the Elementary Grades.* Park Ridge, Ill.: N. A. Kjos Music Co., 1961.

Rolland, P., and M. Mutschler. *The Teaching of Action in String Playing.* Urbana, Ill.: Illinois String Research Associates, 1974.

Runkle, Aleta, and Mary Eriksen. *Music for Today,* 3rd ed. Boston, Mass.: Allyn and Bacon, 1976.

Sacher, Jack, and James Eversole. *The Art of Sound: An Introduction to Music.* Englewood Cliffs, N.J.: Prentice-Hall, Inc., 1971.

Saffran, Rosanna B. *First Book of Creative Rhythms.* New York: Holt, Rinehart and Winston, Inc., 1963.

Schafer, Murray R. *Creative Music Education.* New York: Schirmer Books, 1976.

Schafer, Murray R. *The Composer in the Classroom.* Toronto, Canada: BMI Canada, 1965.

Schafer, Murray R. *Ear Cleaning.* Toronto, Canada: BMI Canada Ltd., 1969.

Schafer, Murray R. *The New Soundscope.* Con Miles, Canada: BMI Canada Ltd., 1969.

Schubert, Inez. *The Craft of Music Teaching in the Elementary School.* Morristown, N.J.: Silver Burdett Company, 1976.

Schwadron, Abraham A. *Aesthetics: Dimensions for Music Education.* Washington, D.C.: Music Educators National Conference, 1967.

Sheehy, Emma Dickson. *There's Music in Children.* New York: Holt, Rinehart and Winston, 1946.

Sidnell, Robert. *Building Instructional Programs in Music Education.* Englewood Cliffs, N.J.: Prentice-Hall, 1973.

Slind, Lloyd H. *Bringing Music to Children: Music Methods for the Elementary School Teacher.* New York: Harper & Row Publishers, 1964.

Smith, Robert B. *Music in the Child's Education.* New York: Ronald Press, 1970.

Swanson, Bessie R. *Music in the Education of Children.* Belmont, Cal.: Wadsworth Publishing Co., 1969.

Swanson, Bessie R. *Planning Music in the Education of Children: A Personal Handbook.* Belmont, Cal.: Wadsworth Publishing Co., 1965.

Swift, Frederic F. *Together We Sing and Play.* New York: Marks Music Corp., 1964.

Timmerman, Maurine, and Celeste Griffith. *Guitar in the Classroom.* Dubuque, Iowa: Wm. C. Brown Co. Publishers, 1976.

Timmerman, Maurine. *Let's Teach Music in the Elementary School.* Evanston, Ill.: Summy-Birchard Publishing Co., 1958.

Ulrich, Homer. *Music, A Design for Listening,* 3rd ed. New York: Harcourt Brace Jovanovich, 1970.

Van Ess, Donald H. *A Listener's Guide to the Heritage of Musical Style.* New York: Holt, Rinehart and Winston, 1970.

Wager, Willis J., and Earl J. McGrath. *Liberal Education and Music.* New York: Bureau of Publications, Teachers College, Columbia University, 1963.

Wilhort, Virginia. *A Teacher's Guide for Use of Handbells in Elementary Music Education.* New York: Harold Flammer, Inc., 1968.

Winslow, Robert W, and Dallin Winslow. *Music Skills for Classroom Teachers,* 4th ed. Dubuque, Iowa: Wm. C. Brown Co. Publishers, 1975.

Wisler, Gene C. *Music Fundamentals for the Classroom Teacher,* 2nd ed. Boston, Mass.: Allyn and Bacon, Inc., 1965.

Words, Sounds and Pictures About Music: A Multimedia Resource Listing for Teachers of Music in Grades K-6. Albany, New York: University of the State of New York, State Education Department, Bureau of Elementary Curriculum Development, 1972.

Worthing, Michell Gratis. *Elements of Music: A Programmed Approach.* Dubuque, Iowa: Wm. C. Brown Co. Publishers, 1977.

Articles

Benn, Oleta. "Excellence in Elementary Music Programs." *Music Educators Journal, 49*(2), 1962, p. 34.

Benner, C. H. "Music Education in a Changing Society." *Music Educators Journal, 61*(9), 1975, p. 32.

Bennett, M. D. "Make the Top 40 Work for You." *Music Educators Journal, 61*(5), 1975, p. 32.

Boberg, Robert M. "Ear-opening Experiences with Rhythm and Pitch." *Music Educators Journal, 62*(4), 1975, p. 32.

Brand, Manny. "Watch What You're Doing." *Music Educators Journal, 63*(3), 1976, p. 50.

Broudy, Harry S. "Does Music Education Need a Philosophy?" *Music Educators Journal, 44*(2), 1957, p. 28.

Cappon, C. "Learning to Listen, Listening to Learn." *Music Educators Journal, 60*(5), 1974, p. 40.

Carle, Irmgard L., and Isaiah Martin. "Enlarge Your Sound Repertory." *Music Educators Journal, 62*(4), 1975, p. 40.

Carlsen, J. C. "Concept Learning—It Starts with a Concept of Music." *Music Educators Journal, 60*(3), 1973, p. 34.

Caylor, Florence. "On the Treadmill of Elementary Music Education." *Music Educators Journal, 58*(7), 1972, p. 33.

Choate, Robert A., and Max Kaplan. "Music in American Society: Introduction to Issues." *Music Educators Journal, 53*(8), p. 43.

Collier, Nina. "Lady in Pink: Modern Dance in Elementary Schools." *Music Educators Journal, 54*(8), 1968, p. 59.

Colwell, Richard. "The Theory of Expectation Applied to Music Listening." *Council for Research in Music Education, 5,* 1965, p. 17.

Cowden, R. L. "A Comparison of First and Third Position Approaches to Violin Instruction." *Journal of Research in Music Education, 20,* 1972, p. 505.

Crist, Christine, Jon Dunn, and Robert Revicki. "Song as a Measure of Man." *Music Educators Journal, 62*(9), 1976, p. 26.

DiRocco, Theresa Sister. "The Child and the Aesthetics of Music." *Music Educators Journal, 55*(8), 1969, p. 34.

Edwards, L. W. "Elementary School Students Should Make Value Judgments." *Music Educators Journal, 61*(1), 1974, p. 41.

Eisman, Lawrence. "Teaching the Difficult General Music Class." *Music Educators Journal, 53*(3), 1966, p. 51.

Esselstrom, Michael J. "Listening Comes Alive in Classroom Concerts." *Music Educators Journal, 57*(8), 1971, p. 44.

Evenson, Flavis. "How Music Concepts Are Applied." *Music Educators Journal, 56*(6), 1970, p. 54.

Feinberg, S. "Creative Problem-solving and the Music Listening Experience." *Music Educators Journal, 61*(1), 1974, p. 53.

Fowler, C. B. "Modular Music Programs—An Alternative to General Music." *Music Educators Journal, 60*(6), 1974, p. 34.

Gaston, E. Thayer. "Aesthetic Experiences in Music." *Music Educators Journal, 49*(6), 1963, p. 25.

Gilbert, Janet P. "Mainstreaming in Your Classroom: What to Expect." *Music Educators Journal, 63*(6), 1977, p. 64.

Gonzo, Carroll. "Aesthetic Experiences: A Coming of Age in Music Education." *Music Educators Journal, 58*(4), 1971, p. 34.

Hoem, Jean C. "Don't Dump the Students Who Can't Do." *Music Educators Journal, 58*(8), 1972, p. 29.

Holt, Dennis M., and Betty R. Flinchum. "Feel the Sound." *Music Educators Journal,* 63(4), 1976, p. 51.

Jacobs, C. "An Investigation of Kinesthetics in Violin Playing." *Journal of Research in Music Education, 17,* 1969, p. 112.

Kaplan, Don. "The Joys of Noise." *Music Educators Journal, 62*(6), 1976, p. 36.

Kinney, Guy. "Elementary Instrumental Program? Yes!" *Music Journal, 31*(1), 1973, p. 12.

Kortkamp, Ivan. "Yodel Up to a Better Register." *Music Educators Journal, 55*(8), 1969, p. 50.

Landor, Ronald A. "Wasting the Intelligence of Every Child." *Music Educators Journal, 58*(9), 1972, p. 40.

Larson, R. C. "Behaviors and Values: Creating a Synthesis. *Music Educators Journal, 60*(2), 1973, p. 40.

Lewis, P. A. "Students Choice." *Music Educators Journal, 60*(6), 1974, p. 38.

Mankin, Linda. "Are We Starting Too Late?" *Music Educators Journal, 55*(8), 1969, p. 36.

McDonald, Dorothy. "Individualizing Music Instruction in the Elementary Schools." *Iowa Music Educator,* December, 1971.

Mead, Margaret. "Music Is a Human Need." *Music Educators Journal, 59*(2), 1972, p. 24.

MENC. "Musical Competencies for Classroom Teachers: An Initial Report from Task Group IV of the MENC Commission on Teacher Education." *Music Educators Journal, 57*(9), 1971, p. 40.

Miessner, W. Otto. "How to Master Rhythms." *Music Educators Journal, 53*(3), 1966, p. 48.

Nash, Grace C. "Music in the Elementary Classroom." *Music, 22* (5), 1970, p. 39.

Neidlinger, Robert J. "Bringing Learning Theory to the Listening Lesson." *Music Educators Journal, 58*(7), 1972, p. 52.

O'Brien, James P. "How Conceptual Learning Takes Place." *Music Educators Journal,* *58*(1), 1971, p. 34.

Oliphant, Robert. "Music and Language: A New Look at an Old Analogy." *Music Educators Journal,* *58*(7), 1972, p. 60.

Olson, Rees. "Teaching Music Concepts by the Discovery Method." *Music Educators Journal,* *54*(1), 1967, p. 51.

"On Teaching Music to the Young Child." *Music Educators Journal,* *55*(8), 1969, p. 33.

Peotter, J. "Contracts." *Music Educators Journal,* *61*(6), 1975, p. 46.

Puopolo, V. "The Development and Experimental Application of Self-instructional Practice Materials for Beginning Instrumentalists." *Journal of Research in Music Education, 19,* 1971, p. 342.

Reese, Sam. "How Do Your Ideas About Music Affect Your Teaching?" *Music Educators Journal,* *62*(6), 1976, p. 84.

Regelski, T. A. "A Ride on the Dialectic Seesaw." *Music Educators Journal,* *61*(7), 1975, p. 28.

Reimer, Bennett. "General Music for the Black Ghetto Child." *Music Educators Journal,* *56*(5), 1970, p. 94.

Reimer, Bennett. "Patterns for the Future." *Music Educators Journal,* *63*(4), 1976, p. 22.

Reynolds, Jane. "Music Outlines for Elementary Teachers." *Music Educators Journal,* *53*(4), 1966, p. 44.

Roach, D. W. "Contemporary Music Education: A Comprehensive Outlook." *Music Educators Journal,* *60*(1), 1973, p. 36.

Robison, Doris E. "There's Therapy in Rhythm." *Music Educators Journal,* *57*(7), 1971, p. 42.

Rogers, V. R. "Open Education: Where Is It Now? Where Is It Heading?" *Music Educators Journal,* *60*(8), 1974, p. 20.

Rolland, P., and R. Colwell. "Development and Trial of a Two-Year Program in String Instruction." *Council for Research in Music Education, 8,* 1966, p. 36.

Rosenkranz, P. A. "Perceptual-Motor Development: Are You Doing Your Part?" *Music Educators Journal,* 61(4), 1974, p. 57.

Rowen, Betty J. "Let Them Move." *Music Educators Journal,* 55(8), 1969, p. 43.

Russell-Smith, Geoffry. "Music—The Key to Education." *Music Educators Journal,* 54(3), 1967, p. 43.

Sand, Ole. "Schools for the Seventies." *Music Educators Journal,* 52(6), 1966, p. 40.

Schmidt, L. "The Process of Music Education." *Music Educators Journal,* 61(6), 1975, p. 50.

Schmitt, Sister Cecilia. "The Thought-Life of the Young Child." *Music Educators Journal,* 58(4), 1971, p. 22.

Schwadron, A. "Are We Ready for Aesthetic Education?" *Music Educators Journal,* 60(2), 1973, p. 36.

Schwadron, A. "In Defense of the Special Music Teacher." *Music Educators Journal,* 52(1), 1965, p. 62.

Slaughter, C. H. "Those Dissonant Boys." *Music Educators Journal,* 52(4), 1966, p. 110.

"The Sounds of Children: The White House Conference on Children." *Music Educators Journal,* 57(7), 1971, p. 47.

Stecher, Miriam B., and Hugh McElheny. "The Structure of Music Can Box a Child In." *Music Educators Journal,* 56(8), 1970, p. 54.

Stene, Elin J. "There Are No Monotones." *Music Educators Journal,* 55(8), 1969, p. 46.

Tait, Malcolm J. "Involving the Young Child in Music: Whisper, Growls, Screams, and Puffs . . . Lead to Composition." *Music Educators Journal,* 57(6), 1971, p. 33.

Tait, Malcolm J. "World Musics: Balancing Our Attitudes and Strategies." *Music Educators Journal,* 61(8), 1975, p. 28.

Uhl, Gladys. "Singing Helps Children Learn How to Read." *Music Educators Journal,* 56(4), 1969, p. 45.

Van Bodegraven, Paul. "Music Education in Transition." *Music Educators Journal,* *51*(6), 1965, p. 26.

Watson, P. "Discovery and Inquiry—Techniques of the New Breed of Learner." *Music Educators Journal,* *61*(5), 1975, p. 50.

Widoe, Russ. "Reviving the Troubadour Tradition." *Music Educators Journal,* *62*(5), 1976, p. 72.

Williams, J. Jerome. "Toward an Effective Elementary Music Program." *North Carolina Music Educator,* February, 1973.

Wollner, Gertrude. "Improvisation in the Elementary Classroom." *Music Educators Journal,* *54*(8), 1968, p. 42.

Woodruff, Asahel. "How Music Concepts Are Developed." *Music Educators Journal,* *56*(6), 1970, p. 51.

Zimmerman, Marilyn Pflederer. "Percept and Concept: Implications of Piaget." *Music Educators Journal,* *56*(6), 1970, p. 49.

GENERAL EDUCATION BOOKS

Adams, Don (ed.). *Education in National Development.* New York: David McKay Company, Inc., 1971.

Adams, Don, and Gerald Reagan. *Schooling and Social Change in Modern America.* New York: David McKay Company, Inc., 1972.

Bandura, Albert. *Principles of Behavior Modification.* New York: Holt, Rinehart and Winston, 1969.

Becker, Wesley C. *An Empirical Basis for Change in Education.* Chicago, Ill.: SRA, Inc., 1971.

Becker, Wesley C. *Parents Are Teachers.* Champaign, Ill.: Research Press, 1971.

Becker, Wesley C., and Sigfried Engleman. *Teaching: An Applied Course in Psychology.* Chicago, Ill.: SRA, Inc., 1972.

Berg, Ivar. *Education and Jobs: The Great Training Robbery.* New York: Praeger Publishers, 1970.

Bijou, S. W., and D. M. Baer (eds.). *Child Development: Readings in Experimental Analysis.* New York: Appleton-Century-Crofts, 1967.

Blackham, G., and A. Silberman. *Modification of Child Behavior: Principles and Procedures.* Belmont, Cal.: Wadsworth Publishing Co., 1970.

Blackie, John. *Inside the Primary School.* New York: Schocken Books, 1971.

Brookover, Wilbur B., and Edsel L. Erickson. *Society, Schools, and Learning.* Boston: Allyn and Bacon, 1969.

Broudy, Harry S. *Democracy and Excellence in American Secondary Education.* Chicago, Ill.: Rand McNally, 1964.

Brown, Claude. *Manchild in the Promised Land.* New York: Macmillan, 1965.

Bruner, Jerome S. *On Knowing: Essays for the Left Hand.* New York: Atheneum, 1965.

Bruner, Jerome S. *The Process of Education.* New York: Vintage Books, 1960.

Bruner, Jerome S. *Toward a Theory of Instruction.* Cambridge, Mass.: Belknap Press, 1966.

Buckley, Nancy K., and Hill M. Walker. *Modifying Classroom Behavior: A Manual of Procedure for Classroom Teachers.* Champaign, Ill.: Research Press, 1971.

Caldwell, Bettye M., and Henry N. Ricciuti. *Review of Child Development Research.* Chicago: University of Chicago Press, 1973.

Carnoy, Martin (ed.). *Schooling in a Corporate Society.* New York: David McKay Company, Inc., 1972.

Chesler, Mark, and Robert Fox. *Role Playing Methods in the Classroom.* Chicago, Ill.: SRA, Inc., 1966.

Clark, Leonard, and Irving Starr. *Secondary School Teaching Methods.* New York: Macmillan, 1967.

Conroy, Pat. *The Water Is Wide.* Boston: Houghton Mifflin Company, 1972.

Dennison, George. *The Lives of Children.* New York: Random House, 1969.

Dinkmeyer, Don, and Rudolf Dreikurs. *Encouraging Children to Learn.* Englewood Cliffs, N.J.: Prentice-Hall, Inc., 1963.

Dreeben, Robert. *On What Is Learned in School.* Reading, Mass.: Addison-Wesley, 1968.

Dreikurs, Rudolf. *Children: The Challenge.* New York: Hawthorn Books, 1964.

Dreikurs, Rudolf. *Psychology in the Classroom.* New York: Harper & Row Publishers, 1968.

Drews, Elizabeth Monroe. *Learning Together.* Englewood Cliffs, N.J.: Prentice-Hall, Inc., 1972

Drucker, Peter F. *Age of Discontinuity: Guidelines to Our Changing Society.* New York: Harper & Row Publishers, 1969.

Elkins, David, and John Flavell (eds.). *Studies in Cognitive Development.* New York: Oxford University Press, 1969.

Featherstone, Joseph. *Schools Where Children Learn.* New York: Liveright, 1971.

Furth, H. G. *Piaget and Knowledge.* Englewood Cliffs, N.J.: Prentice-Hall, Inc., 1969.

Gagne, Robert M. *The Conditions of Learning.* New York: Holt, Rinehart and Winston, 1966.

Gallagher, James. *Teaching the Gifted Child.* Boston, Mass.: Allyn and Bacon, 1964.

Gardner, John W. *Excellence.* New York: Harper & Row Publishers, 1961.

Gardner, John W. *Self-Renewal.* New York: Harper & Row Publishers, 1964.

Ginott, Haim. *Between Parent and Child.* New York: Macmillan, 1965.

Ginott, Haim. *Between Parent and Teenager.* New York: Macmillan, 1969.

Ginott, Haim. *Teacher and Child.* New York: Macmillan, 1972.

Ginsberg, H., and S. Opper. *Piaget's Theory of Intellectual Development.* Englewood Cliffs, N.J.: Prentice-Hall, Inc., 1969.

Glasser, William. *Schools without Failure.* New York: Harper & Row Publishers, 1969.

Glasser, William. *Reality Therapy.* New York: Harper & Row Publishers, 1965.

Goodman, Paul. *Compulsory Mis-education and the Community of Scholars.* New York: Vintage Books, 1964.

Gosciewski, F. William. *Effective Child Rearing: The Behaviorally Aware Parent.* New York: Human Sciences Press, 1976.

Gross, Beatrice, and Ronald Gross. *Radical School Reform.* New York: Simon and Schuster, 1969.

Hall, R. Vance. *Managing Behavior, Parts I, II and III.* Merriam, Kansas: H & H Enterprise, Inc., 1970.

Hamblin, Robert L., David Buckholdt, *et al. The Humanization Process.* New York: John Wiley & Sons, 1971.

Harris, Thomas, *I'm O.K.—You're O.K.* New York: Harper & Row Publishers, 1969.

Haslam, Robert A., and Peter J. Valetutti. *Medical Problems in the Classroom.* Baltimore: University Park Press, 1975.

Herndon, James. *The Way It Spozed to Be.* New York: Simon and Schuster, 1968.

Hertzberg, Alvin, and Edward F. Stone. *Schools Are for Children: An American Approach to the Open Classroom.* New York: Schocken Books, 1971.

Holt, John. *How Children Fail.* New York: Pitman Publishing Corp., 1964.

Holt, John. *How Children Learn.* New York: Pitman Publishing Corp., 1967.

Holt, John. *The Underachieving School.* New York: Pitman Publishing Corp., 1969.

Holt, John. *What Do I Do on Monday?.* New York: Dutton, 1970.

Homme, Lloyd. *How to Use Contingency Contracting in the Classroom.* Champaign, Ill.: Research Press, 1969.

Howes, Virgil. *Individualization of Instruction.* New York: Macmillan, 1970.

Illich, Ivan. *Deschooling Society.* New York: Harper & Row Publishers, 1971.

Inhelder, B., and J. Piaget. *The Growth of Logical Thinking from Childhood to Adolescence.* New York: Basic Books, 1958.

Jones, Richard. *Fantasy and Feeling in Education.* New York: University Press, 1968.

Kagan, Jerome (ed.). *Creativity and Learning.* Boston, Mass.: Houghton Mifflin, 1967.

Koch, Kenneth. *Wishes, Lies, and Dreams.* New York: Chelsea House Publishing Co., 1970.

Kohl, Herbert. *The Open Classroom.* New York: Random House, 1969.

Kohl, Herbert. *36 Children.* New York: New American Library, 1967.

Kozol, Jonathan. *Death at an Early Age.* Boston, Mass.: Houghton Mifflin, 1967.

Kozol, Jonathan. *The Night Is Dark and I Am Far from Home.* New York: Bantam Books, 1975.

Leonard, George. *Education and Ecstasy.* New York: Delacorte Press, 1968.

Long, Nicholas J., William C. Morse, and Ruth G. Newman (eds.). *Conflict in the Classroom.* Belmont, Cal.: Wadsworth Publishing Co., 1965.

McIntire, Roger W. *For Love of Children: Behavioral Psychology for Parents.* Del Mar: CRM Books, 1970.

Madsen, C. K., and C. H. Madsen. *Parents and Children: Love and Discipline; A Positive Guide to Behavior Modification.* Arlington Heights, Illinois: AHM, 1975.

Madsen, C. K., and C. H. Madsen. *Teaching/Discipline: A Positive Approach for Educational Development.* Boston, Mass.: Allyn and Bacon, 1974.

Mager, Robert. *Developing Attitudes Toward Learning.* Belmont, Cal.: Fearon Publishers, 1966.

Mager, Robert. *Preparing Instructional Objectives.* Belmont, Cal.: Fearon Publishers, 1962.

Meachan, M. L., and A. E. Wiesen. *Changing Classroom Behavior: A Manual for Precision Techniques.* Scranton, Pa.: International Textbook Co., 1969.

Mink, O. G. *The Behavior Change Process.* New York: Harper & Row Publishers, 1968.

Muenzinger, Karl F. *Contemporary Approaches to Creative Thinking.* New York: Atherton Press, 1967.

Neill, Alexander S. *Summerhill.* New York: Hart Publishing Co., 1960.

Osborn, A. *Applied Imagination.* New York: Charles Scribner's Sons, 1957.

Parnes, I. J. *Creative Behavior Workbook.* New York: Charles Scribner's Sons, 1967.

Patrick, Catherine. *What Is Creativity Thinking?* New York: Philosophical Library, 1955.

Patterson, Gerald R., and M. Elizabeth Guillon. *Living with Children.* Champaign, Ill.: Research Press, 1968.

Payne, James S., Edward A. Polloway, James M. Kauffman, and T. R. Scranton. *Living in the Classroom.* New York: Human Sciences Press, 1976.

Phillips, J. L. *The Origins of Intellect.* San Francisco, Cal.: W. H. Freeman, 1969.

Postman, Neil, and Charles Weingartner. *The Soft Revolution.* New York: Delacorte Press, 1971.

Postman, Neil, and Charles Weingartner. *Teaching as a Subversive Activity.* New York: Delacorte Press, 1969.

Raths, Louis, Merrill Harmin, and Sidney Simon. *Values and Teaching.* Columbus, Ohio: Charles E. Merrill Books, 1966.

Rogers, Carl. *Freedom to Learn.* Columbus, Ohio: Charles E. Merrill Publishing Co., 1969.

Rogers, Carl. *On Becoming a Person.* Boston, Mass.: Houghton Mifflin, 1961.

Rosenthal, R., and L. Jacobson. *Pygmalion in the Classroom: Teacher Expectations and Pupils Intellectual Development.* New York: Holt, Rinehart and Winston, 1968.

Russell, Bertrand. *Education and the Good Life.* New York: Avon Book Division, 1926.

Schmuck, Richard, Mark Chesler, and Ronald Lippitt. *Problem Solving to Improve Classroom Learning.* Chicago, Ill.: SRA, Inc., 1966.

Shumsky, Abraham. *Creative Teaching in the Elementary School.* New York: Appleton-Century-Crofts, 1969.

Skinner, B. F. *The Technology of Teaching.* New York: Appleton-Century-Crofts, 1968.

Silberman, Charles E. *Crises in the Classroom.* New York: Random House, 1970.

Silberman, Melvin L. (ed.). *The Experience of Schooling.* New York: Holt, Rinehart and Winston, 1971.

Smith, James A. *Setting Conditions for Creative Teaching in the Elementary School.* Boston, Mass.: Allyn and Bacon, 1966.

Staats, Arthur W. *Learning, Language, and Cognition.* New York: Holt, Rinehart and Winston, 1968.

Staats, Arthur W. *Social Behaviorism.* Homewood, Ill.: Dorsey Press, 1975.

Torrance, E. P. *Guiding Creative Talent.* Englewood Cliffs, N.J.: Prentice-Hall, Inc., 1962.

Thut, I. N., and D. Adams. *Patterns of Education in Contemporary Societies.* New York: McGraw-Hill, 1964.

RESOURCES FOR EXCEPTIONAL CHILDREN

REFERENCES

"A C/P Child is in Your Class." Free brochure. National Cystic Fibrosis Research Foundation, 202 E. 44th Street, New York, New York 10017.

Alvin, Juliette. *Music for the Handicapped Child.* New York: Oxford University Press, 1965.

Alvin, Juliette. *Music Therapy.* New York: Oxford University Press, 1966.

Becker, Wesley C. (ed.). *An Empirical Basis for Change in Education.* Chicago, Ill.: SRA, Inc., 1971.

Becker, Wesley C., S. Engelmann, and Don R. Thomas. *Teaching: A Course in Applied Psychology.* Chicago, Ill.: SRA, Inc., 1971.

Bender, Michael, and Peter J. Vallettutti. *Teaching the Moderately and Severely Handicapped.* Baltimore: University Park Press, 1976.

"Cerebral Palsy—What You Should Know About It." Free brochure. United C-P Association, Inc., 66 East 34th Street, New York, New York 10016.

Cruickshank, William, et al. *Misfits in the Public Schools.* Syracuse, New York: Syracuse University Press, 1969.

Dobbs, J. P. B. *The Slow Learner and Music.* New York: Oxford University Press, 1966.

Dunn, Lloyd. *Exceptional Children in the Schools.* New York: Holt, Rinehart and Winston, 1966.

Eagle, Charles T. (ed.). *Music Therapy Index: An International Interdisciplinary Index to the Literature of the Psychology, Psychophysiology, Psychophysics and Sociology of Music* (Volume 1). Lawrence, Kansas: National Association for Music Therapy, Inc., 1976.

Erickson, Marion J. *The Mentally Retarded Child in the Classroom.* New York: Macmillan, 1965.

Frankel, Max, William Happ, and Maurice Smith. *Functional Teaching of the Mentally Retarded.* Springfield, Ill.: Charles Thomas, 1966.

Frostig, Marianne. *Move, Grow, Learn.* Chicago, Ill.: Follett Publishing Co.

Gaston, E. Thayer. *Music in Therapy.* New York: Macmillan., 1968.

Gordon, Edwin. "The Use of the Musical Aptitude Profile with Exceptional Children." *Journal of Music Therapy, 5*(2), 1968, p. 37.

Graham, Richard M. (ed.). *Music for the Exceptional Child.* Reston, Virginia: Music Educators National Conference, 1975.

Gray, Vera, and Rachel Percival. *Music, Movement and Mime.* New York: Oxford University Press, 1962.

Greer, R. Douglas, and Laura G. Dorow. *Specializing Education Behaviorally.* Dubuque, Iowa: Kendall-Hunt Publishing Co., 1976.

Hewett, Frank M. *The Emotionally Disturbed Child in the Classroom.* Boston, Mass.: Allyn and Bacon, 1968.

Hill, John D. "The Musical Achievement of Culturally Deprived and Advantaged Children: A Comparative Study at the Elementary Level." *Journal of Music Therapy, 5*(3), 1968, p. 77.

Hood, Marguerite. *Teaching Rhythms and Using Instruments.* Englewood Cliffs, N.J.: Prentice-Hall, Inc., 1970.

How They Hear. Northbrook, Ill.: Gordon Stowe Association.

Johnson, Doris, and Helmer R. Myklebust. *Learning Disabilities, Educational Principles and Practices.* New York: Grune and Stratton, 1967.

Johnson, W., and Dorothy Moellner (eds.). *Speech Handicapped School Children.* New York: Harper & Row Publishers, 1967.

Kephart, N. *The Slow Learner in the Classroom.* Columbus, Ohio: Charles E. Merrill Publishing Co., 1960.

Kirk, Samuel. *Educating Exceptional Children.* Boston, Mass.: Houghton Mifflin Co, 1972.

Kirk, Samuel. *The Education of Exceptional Children.* Chicago: University of Chicago Press, 1950.

Lewis, Richard S., Alfred A. Strauss, and Laura E. Lehtinen. *The Other Child.* New York: Grune and Stratton, 1960.

Madsen, C. K., R. D. Greer, and C. H. Madsen (eds.). *Research in Music Behavior.* New York: Columbia University Teachers College Press, 1975.

Madsen, C. H., Jr., and C. K. Madsen. *Teaching/Discipline: A Positive Approach for Educational Development.* Boston, Mass.: Allyn and Bacon, 1974.

Music for Special Education. Washington, D.C.: MENC, 1201 16th Street.

Nordoff, Paul, and Clive Robbins. *Music Therapy for Handicapped Children.* New York: Rudolf Steiner Publications, 1965.

Nordoff, Paul, and Clive Robbins. *Music Therapy in Special Education.* New York: John Day Co., 1971.

Nordoff, Paul, and Clive Robbins. *Therapy in Music for Handicapped Children.* New York: St. Martin's Press, 1972.

Pelone, A. J. *Helping the Visually Handicapped Child in a Regular Class.* New York: Columbia University Teachers College Press, 1957.

Purvis, Jennie, and Shelley Samet (eds.). *Music in Developmental Therapy.* Baltimore: University Park Press, 1976.

O'Leary, K. D., and S. G. O'Leary. *Classroom Management.* New York: Pergammon Press, Inc., 1972.

Perry, Natalie. *Teaching the Mentally Retarded Child.* New York: Columbia University Press, 1960.

Robins, Ferris, and Jennet Robins. *Educational Rhythmics for Mentally and Physically Handicapped Children.* New York: Association Press, 1968.

Rubella. PHS Publication No. 2041, U.S. Dept. HEW, 1970. Superintendent of Documents, U.S. Government Printing Office, Washington, D.C. 20402.

Schattner, Regina. *Creative Dramatics for Handicapped Children.* New York: John Day Co., 1967.

Telford, Charles, and James Sawrey. *The Exceptional Individual.* Englewood Cliffs, N.J.: Prentice-Hall, Inc., 1967.

Torrance, E. Paul. *Gifted Children in the Classroom.* New York: Macmillan Co., 1965.

What Research Says to the Teacher Series. NEA, 1201 16th Street N.W., Washington, D.C. 20036.

What Teacher Should Know About Children with Heart Disease. Free brochure. American Heart Association, 44 E. 23rd Street, New York, New York 10010.

Wood, Mary M. (ed.). *Developmental Therapy.* Baltimore: University Park Press, 1975.

INSTRUCTIONAL BOOKS

Andrews, Gladys. *Creative Rhythmic Movement for Children.* Englewood Cliffs, N.J.: Prentice-Hall, Inc., 1954.

Avery, R., and D. Marsh. *Hymns Hot and Carols Cool.* New York: Proclamation Productions, 7 Kingston Avenue, Port Jervis 12771.

Cole, Frances. *Music for Children with Special Needs.* North Hollywood, Cal.: Bowmar Records, Inc., 10505 Burbank Blvd.

Coleman, Jack, Irene Schoepfle, and Virginia Templeton. *Music for Exceptional Children.* Evanston, Ill.: Summy-Birchard Co, 1964.

Dance-A-Story. New York: Ginn and Co., 1964.

Doll, Edna, and Mary Nelson. *Rhythms Today.* Morristown, N.J.: Silver Burdett Co., 1965.

Gant, Elizabeth, and Katherine Gant. *Rip Van Winkle.* Nashville, Tenn.: Abingdon Press, 1969.

Gant, Elizabeth, and Katherine Gant. *Little Red Riding Hood.* Nashville, Tenn.: Abingdon Press.

Hap Palmer Songbook. Freeport, New York: Educational Activities.

Laurence, Ester Hansen. *Catch a Dragon.* Nashville, Tenn.: Abingdon Press, 1969.

Mandell, Muriel, and Robert Wood. *Make Your Own Musical Instruments.* New York: Sterling Publishing Co., Inc., 1959.

Moss, Jeffrey, and Joe Raposo. *Sesame Street Songbook.* New York: Simon and Schuster, 1971

Nordoff, Paul, and Clive Robbins. *Artaban, The Other Wiseman.* Bryn Mawr, Pa.: Theodore Presser Co., 1968.

Nordoff, Paul, and Clive Robbins. *The Children's Christmas Play.* Bryn Mawr, Pa.: Theodore Presser Co., 1965.

Nordoff, Paul, and Clive Robbins. *Children's Playsongs.* Bryn Mawr, Pa.: Theodore Presser Co., 1964.

Nordoff, Paul, and Clive Robbins. *Children's Playsongs with Resonator Bells.* Bryn Mawr, Pa.: Theodore Presser Co., 1965.

Nordoff, Paul, and Clive Robbins. *Fun for Four Drums.* Bryn Mawr, Pa.: Theodore Pressor Co., 1965.

Nordoff, Paul, and Clive Robbins. *Pif, Paf, Poltrie.* Bryn Mawr, Pa.: Theodore Presser Co., 1961.

Nordoff, Paul, and Clive Robbins. *Spirituals for Children to Sing and Play.* Bryn Mawr, Pa.: Theodore Presser Co., 1971.

Nordoff, Paul, and Clive Robbins. *The Three Bears.* Bryn Mawr, Pa.: Theodore Presser Co., 1966.

Roberts, Ronald. *Musical Instruments Made to be Played.* Leicester, England: Dryad Press.

Saffran, Rosanna. *First Book of Creative Rhythms.* New York: Holt, Rinehart and Winston, 1963.

Schattner, Regina. *Creative Dramatics for Handicapped Children.* New York: John Day Co., 1967.

Seeger, Ruth Crawford. *American Folksongs for Children.* Garden City, New York: Doubleday & Co., 1948.

Up With People Songbook. Dayton, Ohio: Lorenz Publishing Co.

Walt Disney Favorites. Miami Beach, Fla.: Hansen Publications, Inc.

Weber, Richard. *Musicall.* New York: Musicall, Inc.

MATERIALS

American Guidance Service, Inc., Publisher's Building, Circle Pines, Minnesota, 55014.

Childcraft Education Corporation, 20 Kilmer Road, P. O. Box 500, Edison, New Jersey, 08817

Developmental Learning Materials, 7440 Natchez Avenue, Niles, Illinois, 60648.

Educational Activities, Inc., P. O. Box 392, Freeport, New York, 11520.

R. H. Stone Products, 13735 Puritan, Detroit, Michigan, 48227.

ELEMENTARY MUSIC SERIES

Addison-Wesley. Menlo Park, Cal. *Comprehensive Musicianship.* (Hawaii Music Program Curriculum Research and Development Group). K-12, 1974.

Allyn and Bacon, Inc. 470 Atlantic Ave., Boston, Mass. 02210. *This Is Music for Today.* K-8, 1971.

American Book Co. 450 West 33rd St., New York, N.Y. 10001. *Music For Young Americans.* 1 8, 1966.

American Book Co. 450 West 33rd St., New York, N.Y. 10001. *New Dimensions in Music,* 1970.

Follett Publishing Co. 1010 West Washington Blvd., Chicago, Ill. 60607. *Discovering Music Together.* K-8, 1966.

Ginn and Co. 191 Spring St., Lexington, Mass. 02173. *The Magic of Music.* K-8, 1969.

Holt, Rinehart and Winston. 383 Madison Ave., New York, N.Y. 10017. *Exploring Music.* K-8, and the Senior Book, 1975.

Macmillan Publishing Co. 255 Ottley Drive, N.E., Atlanta, Ga. 30324. *The Spectrum of Music.* K-8, 1974.

Prentice-Hall, Inc. Englewood Cliffs, N.J. 07732. *Growing with Music.* K-8, 1966.

Silver Burdett Co. 250 James St., Morristown, N. J. 07960. *Making Music Your Own.* K-8, 1968.

Silver Burdett Co. 250 James St., Morristown, N.J. 07960. *Silver Burdett Music.* K-8, 1974.

Summy-Birchard Publishing Co. *Birchard Music Series.* K-8, 1959.

RECORDINGS, FILMS, AND OTHER TEACHING AIDS

RECORDINGS

Ampex Stereo Tape. 65 Commerce Way, Hackensack, N.J.

Angel Records. 1750 North Vine St., Hollywood, Cal. 90028.

Archive of Folk Music. See Everest Records.

Argo Records. Argo Sight and Sound, Ltd. 539 West 25th St., New York, N.Y. 10001.

Atlantic Records. 1841 Broadway, New York, N.Y. 10023.

Avant Garde Records. 250 West 57th St., New York, N.Y. 10019.

Bowmar Records. 622 Rodier Dr., Glendale, Cal.

Burns Record Co. 755 Chickadee Lane, Stratford, Conn.

Camden Records (c/o RCA Records). 1133 Avenue of the Americas, New York, N.Y. 10036.

Candide (c/o Vox Records). 211 East 43rd St., New York, N.Y. 10017.

Capitol Records. 1750 North Vine St., Hollywood, Cal. 90028.

Chess Records. 1301 Avenue of the Americas, New York, N.Y. 10019.

Children's Record Guild (Franson Corporation). 225 Park Ave., New York, N.Y. 10003.

Columbia Records (c/o CBS Records). 51 West 52nd St., New York, N.Y. 10019.

Composers Recordings. 170 West 74th St., New York, N.Y. 10023.

Cotillion (c/o Atlantic Records). 1841 Broadway, New York, N.Y. 10023.

Crescendo Records (c/o GNP—Crescendo Records, Inc.). 9165 Sunset Blvd., Hollywood, Cal. 90069

Decca (c/o MCA, Decca Division). 100 Universal City Plaza, Universal City, Cal. 91608.

Deutsche Grammophon Gesellschaft (c/o Polydor). 1700 Broadway, New York, N.Y. 10019.

Disneyland Records. 800 Sonora Ave., Glendale, Cal. 91201.

Dover Publications. 180 Varick St., New York, N.Y. 10014.

Dunhill Records (c/o ABC Records). 8255 Beverly Blvd., Los Angeles, Cal. 90048.

Educational Activities. P.O. Box 392, Freeport, N.Y. 11520.

Educational Record Sales. 157 Chambers St., New York, N.Y.

Elektra Records. 15 Columbus Circle, New York, N.Y. 10023.

Enterprise Records (c/o Stax Records). 98 North Avalon, Memphis, Tenn. 38104.

Epic Records. 51 West 52nd St., New York, N.Y. 10019.

Era Records. 118 South Beverly Dr., Beverly Hills, Cal. 90212.

Everest Records. 10920 Wilshire Blvd., West Los Angeles, Cal. 90024.

Fame Records (c/o United Artists Records). 6920 Sunset Blvd., Hollywood, Cal. 90028.

Fidelity Sound Recordings. 206–19 Jamaica Ave., Jamaica, N.Y.

Folkways Records Corp. 701 7th Ave., New York, N.Y. 10036.

Folkways/Scholastic. 701 7th Ave., New York, N.Y. 10036.

Fontana Records. 35 East Wacker Dr., Chicago, Ill. 60601.

Four Corners Records. 136 East 57th St., New York, N.Y.

Galaxy Records (c/o Roulette Records). 17 West 60th St., New York, N.Y. 10023.

Golden Children's Records. 250 West 57th St., New York, N.Y. 10019.

Gordy Records (c/o Motown Records). 6464 Sunset Blvd., Hollywood, Cal. 90028.

Hifi Records (c/o Everest Enterprises). 10920 Wilshire Blvd., West Los Angeles, Cal. 90024.

Hula Records. P.O. Box 2135, Honolulu, Hawaii 96805.

Imperial Records (c/o United Artists Records). 6920 Sunset Blvd., Hollywood, Cal. 90028

Indian House Records. P.O. Box 472, Taos, New Mexico 87571.

Janus Records. 1700 Broadway, New York, N.Y. 10019

Kama Sutra Records. 810 7th Ave., New York, N.Y. 10019

Liberty Records, Inc. 1776 Broadway, New York, N.Y. 10019.

London Records. 539 West 25th St., New York, N.Y. 10001.

Lyons. 688 Industrial Dr., Elmhurst, Ill.

Lyrichord Discs. 141 Perry St., New York, N.Y. 10014.

Mercury Records. 35 East Wacker Dr., Chicago, Ill. 60601.

MGM Records. 7165 Sunset Blvd., Los Angeles, Cal. 90046.

Monument Records (c/o CBS Records). 51 West 52nd St., New York, N.Y. 10019.

Motown Records. 6464 Sunset Blvd., Hollywood, Cal. 90028.

Musart Records. 780 West 27th St., Hialeah, Fla. 33010.

Nonesuch Records. 15 Columbus Circle, New York, N.Y. 10023.

Oak Records. 6430 Sunset Blvd., Hollywood, Cal. 90028.

Odyssey Records (c/o Columbia Records). 51 West 52nd St., New York, N.Y. 10019.

Paramount Records (c/o Famous Music Corp.). Gulf and Western Plaza, New York, N.Y. 10023.

Peter Pan Records (c/o Empire State). 10–20 46th Road, Long Island City, N.Y.

Philips Records. 35 East Wacker Dr., Chicago, Ill. 60601.

Polydor. 1700 Broadway, New York, N.Y. 10019.

Rampart Records (c/o Cordo Enterprises). 544 North Western Ave., Los Angeles, Cal. 90004.

RCA Records. 1133 Avenue of the Americas, New York, N.Y. 10036.

Renaissance Records (c/o Everest Enterprises). 10920 Wilshire Blvd., West Los Angeles, Cal. 90024.

Reprise Records (c/o Warner Bros. Records). 4000 Warner Blvd., Burbank, Cal. 91505.

Richmond Records (c/o London Records). 539 West 25th St., New York, N.Y. 10001.

Scepter Records. 254 West 54th St., New York, N.Y. 10019.

Seraphim Records (c/o Capitol Records). 1750 North Vine St., Hollywood, Cal. 90028.

Soul Records (c/o Motown Records). 6464 Sunset Blvd., Hollywood, Cal. 90028.

Southland Records (c/o Jazzology Records). P.O. Box 748, Columbia, S.C. 29202.

Stanley Bowmar Co., Inc. 12 Cleveland St. Valhalla, N.Y.

Stax Records. 98 North Avalon, Memphis, Tenn. 38104.

Sussex Records (c/o Buddah/Kama Sutra). 810 7th Ave., New York, N.Y. 10019.

Tahiti Records. P.O. Box 478, Papeete, Tahiti.

Telefunken (c/o Argo Sight & Sound, Ltd.). 539 West 25th St., New York, N.Y. 10001.

Tiare Tahiti Records. 6124 Selma Ave., Hollywood, Cal. 90028.

Turnabout Records (c/o Vox Records). 211 East 43rd St., New York, N.Y. 10017.

United Artists Records. 6920 Sunset Blvd., Hollywood, Cal. 90028.

Vanguard Recording Society. 71 West 23rd St., New York, N.Y. 10010.

Victor Records (c/o RCA Records). 1133 Avenue of the Americas, New York, N.Y. 10036.

Vista Records. 800 Sonora Ave., Glendale, Cal. 91201.

Vox Productions, Inc. 211 East 43rd St., New York, N.Y. 10017.

Warner Bros. Records. 4000 Warner Blvd., Burbank, Cal. 91505.

Westminster Recording Co. (c/o ABC Records). 8255 Beverly Blvd., Hollywood, Cal. 90028.

World Pacific Records (c/o United Artists Records). 6920 Sunset Blvd., Hollywood, Cal. 90028.

Young People's Records (c/o Franson Corporation). 225 Park Ave., New York, N.Y. 10003.

FILMS AND FILMSTRIPS

Audio-Visual Divison, Inc. 355 Lexington Ave., New York, N.Y.

Bailey Films, Inc. 6509 De Longpre Ave., Los Angeles, Cal.

Bell Telephone System, Motion Picture Section. 195 Broadway, New York, N.Y. 10007.

Bowmar. 622 Rodier Dr., Glendale, Cal. 91201.

Conn Corporation. Elkhart, Ind.

Contemporary Films, Inc. 267 West 25th St., New York, N.Y. 10001.

Coronet Films. 65 E. South Water St., Chicago, Ill.

Encyclopaedia Britannica Films. 1150 Wilmette Ave., Wilmette, Ill.

Eye Gate House, Inc. 146–01 Archer Ave., Jamaica, N.Y.

Film Associates of California. 11559 Santa Monica Blvd., Los Angeles, Cal.

Jam Handy Scott Educational Division. 104 Lower Westfield Road, Holyoke, Mass. 01040.

Keyboard Publication, Inc. 1346 Chapel St., New Haven, Conn. 06511.

McGraw-Hill Book Co., Inc. 330 West 42nd St., New York, N.Y.

Musilog Corporation. P.O. Box 1199, 1600 Anacapa St., Santa Barbara, Cal. 93102.

Society for Visual Education, Inc. 1345 W. Diversey Parkway, Chicago, Ill. 60614.

Swartwout Enterprises. Box 476, Scottsdale, Ariz. 85252.

Walt Disney Motion Pictures. 477 Madison Ave., New York, N.Y. 10017.

TRANSPARENCIES

Educom Ltd. Box 388, Mt. Kisco, N.Y. 10549.

Minnesota Mining and Manufacturing Co. St. Paul, Minn.

ART AND ART PRINTS

Bro-Dart Master Color Prints. 1609 Memorian Ave., Williamsport, Pa.

Giant Photos. Box 406, Rockford, Ill.

Harlem Book Co. 221 Park Ave. South, New York, N.Y.

Erich S. Herrmann, Inc. 3 East 28th St., New York, N.Y.

New York Graphic. 140 Greenwich Ave., Box 1469, Greenwich, Conn.

Oestreicher's Prints, Inc. 43 West 46th St., New York, N.Y.

Perry Pictures Co. Malden, Mass.

Society for Visual Education, Inc. 1345 West Diversey Parkway, Chicago, Ill. 60614

MUSIC

Abelard-Schuman. 6 West 57th St., New York, N.Y.

Associated Music Publishers, Inc. 609 5th Ave., New York, N.Y.

Belwin, Inc. 250 Maple Ave., Rockville Centre, N.Y.

C.F. Peters Corporation. 373 Park Ave. South, New York, N.Y.

Carl Fischer, Inc. 62 Cooper Square, New York, N.Y.

Consolidated Music Publishers, Inc. 33 West 60th St., New York, N.Y.

Edward B. Marks Music Corporation. 136 West 52nd St., New York, N.Y.

G. Ricordi (Franco Colombo). 16 West 61st St., New York, N.Y.

G. Schirmer, Inc. 4 East 49th St., New York, N.Y.

Harold Flammer, Inc. 251 West 19th St., New York, N.Y.

International Music Co. 511 5th Ave., New York, N.Y.

Joseph Patelson Music House, 160 West 56th Street, New York, N.Y.

Lee Roberts Music Publications (c/o G. Schirmer, Inc.). 4 East 49th St., New York, N.Y.

Leeds Music Corporation. 445 Park Ave., New York, N.Y.

M. Witmark & Sons Co. 619 West 54th St., New York, N.Y.

MCA Music, Inc. 543 West 43rd St., New York, N.Y.

Mannorhouse Press. Paris, Tenn.

Miller Music Corporation. 1350 Avenue of the Americas, New York, N.Y.

Sam Fox Publishing Co. 1841 Broadway, New York, N.Y.

Southern Music Co., P. O. Box 329, San Antonio, Texas.

Summy-Birchard Co. 1834 Ridge Ave., Evanston, Ill.

Wadsworth Publishing Co., Inc. 75 Varick St., New York, N.Y.

Webster Publishing Co. Manchester Road, Manchester, Mo.

Willis Music Co. 440 Main St., Cincinnati, Ohio.

CLASSROOM INSTRUMENTS

Children's Music Center. 5373 West Pico Blvd., Los Angeles, Cal. 90019.

T. C. Dragon, Inc. 1770 W. Berteau Ave., Chicago, Ill. 60613.

Educational Music Bureau, Inc. 434 Wabash Ave., Chicago, Ill. 60605.

Gamble Hinged Music Co. 312 South Wabash Ave., Chicago, Ill. 60604.

Goya Music, Division of Avnet, Inc. 53 West 23rd St., New York, N.Y. 10010.

Hargail Music Press. 157 West 57th St., New York, N.Y. 10019.

Harmolin, Inc. P.O. Box 244, La Jolla, Cal. 92037.

Harmony Company. 4600 W. Diversey Ave., Chicago, Ill. 60639.

M. Hohner, Inc. Andrews Road, Hicksville, N.Y. 11802.

Magna-Music Baton, Inc. 6394 Delmar Blvd., St. Louis, Mo 63130.

Melody Flute Co. Laurel, Md. 20810.

Music Education Group. P.O. Box 1501, Union, N.Y. 07083.

Oscar Schmidt-International, Inc. 87–101 Ferry St., Jersey City, N.J. 07307.

Pacific Music Supply Co. 1143 Santee St., Los Angeles, Cal. 90015.

Peripole Products, Inc. 51–17 Rockaway Beach Blvd., Far Rockaway, N.Y. 11691.

Rhythm Band, Inc. Box 126, Fort Worth, Tex. 76101.

Targ-Dinner, Inc. 2451 N. Sacramento St., Chicago, Ill. 60647.

Viking Co. 113 South Edgemount St., Los Angeles, Cal. 90004.

Walberg and Auge. 31 Mercantile St., Worcester, Mass. 01608.

Yamaha International Corporation. Box 54540, Los Angeles, Cal. 90054.

Zim-Gar Musical Instrument Corporation. 762 Park Place, Brooklyn, N.Y. 11216.

MISCELLANEOUS AIDS

Antiseptic and Germicides: Tone Play-Safe Mouth Piece Sanitizer (spray), Virginia Aerosol, Inc., Winchester, Va.

Hula-Hoops: Wham-O Mfg., 835 E. El Monte St., San Gabriel, Cal. 91778.

Making Music Your Own. Large charts of illustrations in K and Book I. Silver Burdett, Morristown, N.J.

MUSIC FOR THE VISUALLY HANDICAPPED

American Printing House for the Blind. Louisville, Ky. Braille and large print music materials, including band, orchestra and choral.

Henkins, Edward. *Braille Music Primer.* American Printing House, Louisville, Ky.

PERIODICALS

Behavior Research and Therapy
Child Development
Council for Basic Education Bulletin
Council for Research in Music Education
ERIC
Exceptional Children
Journal of Applied Behavior Analysis
Journal of Educational Psychology
Review of Educational Research
Journal of Experimental Child Psychology
Journal of Music Therapy
Journal of Research in Music Education
Journal of School Psychology
Journal of Special Education
Music Educators Journal
Psychological Bulletin
Psychology in the Schools
Young Children

DISCOGRAPHY

Adventures in Music. Gladys Tipton (ed.). RCA Victor. 155 East 24th St., New York, N.Y. Twelve albums organized by grade level, each containing a Teacher's Guide booklet.

Balkin, Al. *We Live in the City.* Theodore Presser Co. 1712 Chestnut St., Bryn Mawr, Pa.

Basic Concepts Through Dance for Exceptional Children. Educational Activities, Inc. P.O. Box 392, Freeport, N.Y. 11520.

Bowmar Orchestral Library. Lucille Wood (ed.). Stanley Records. 12 Cleveland St., Valhalla, N.Y. Thirty-six albums with theme charts.

Children's Record Guild and *Young People's Records.* Greystone Corp., Educational Activities Division. 100 6th Ave., New York, N.Y.

Classroom Rhythms: Animal Rhythms. Classroom Materials Co., Great Neck, N.Y.

Dance-a-Long. Ginn and Co. (c/o Xerox College Publishing). 274 Wyman St., Waltham, Mass. 02154.

Dance-a-Story. Ginn and Co. (c/o Xerox College Publishing). 274 Wyman St., Waltham, Mass. 02154.

Educational Records Catalog. RCA Record Division, 155 East 24th St., New York, N.Y.

Jenkins, Ella. *Counting Games and Rhythm for Little Ones.* (FC7056), Folkways Records.

Jenkins, Ella. *You'll Sing a Song and I'll Sing a Song. (FC7056), Folkways Records.*

Me, Myself, and I. Childrens Music Center, Inc. 5373 Pico Blvd., Los Angeles, Cal. 90019.

Music for Young Listeners and *Tiny Masterpieces for Very Young Listeners.* Sound Book Press Society, Inc. P.O. Box 222, Scarsdale, N.Y.

Music Master Series. Vox Productions, Inc. 236 West 55th St., New York, N.Y.

My Playful Scarf. Childrens Music Center, Inc. 5373 Pico Blvd., Los Angeles, Cal. 90019.

Palmer, Hap. *Creative Movement and Rhythmic Exploration.* Educational Activities, Inc. P.O. Box 392, Freeport, N.Y. 11520.

Palmer, Hap. *Folk Song Carnival.* Educational Activities, Inc. P.O. Box 392, Freeport, N.Y. 11520.

Palmer, Hap. *Learning Basic Skills Through Music.* Educational Activities, Inc. P.O. Box 392, Freeport, N.Y. 11520.

Palmer, Hap. *Mod Marches.* Educational Activities, Inc. P.O. Box 392, Freeport, N.Y. 11520.

Palmer, Hap. *Modern Rhythm Band Tunes.* Educational Activities, Inc. P.O. Box 392, Freeport, N.Y. 11520.

Palmer, Hap. *Patriotic and Morning Time Songs.* Educational Activities, Inc. P.O. Box 392, Freeport, N.Y. 11520.

Palmer, Hap. *Simplified Folk Songs.* Educational Activities, Inc. P.O. Box 392, Freeport, N.Y. 11520.

Sing 'n Do Songs. Sing 'n Do Company, Ridgewood, N.J.

SUPPLEMENTARY VOCAL
MATERIALS

Barlow, Betty M. *Do It Yourself Songs.* Delaware Water Gap, Pa.: Shawnee Press, Inc., 1964.

Best, Beth, and Dick Best. *The New Song Fest.* New York: Crown Publishers, Inc., 1966.

Coleman, Satis. *Christmas Carols from Many Countries.* New York: G. Schirmer, Inc., 1934.

Coleman, Satis. *Another Dancing Time.* New York: John Day Co., 1954.

Coleman, Satis. *Another Singing Time.* New York: John Day Co., 1952.

Coleman, Satis. *Songs of American Folks.* New York: John Day Co., 1942.

Crowninshield, Ethel. *Walk the World Together.* Boston, Mass.: The Boston Music Co., 1951.

Daniel, Oliver. *Round and Round They Go.* Boston, Mass.: C. C. Birchard and Co., 1952.

De Cesare, Ruth. *Latin-American Game Songs.* New York: Miles Music, Inc., 1959.

Fassio, A. *French Folk Songs.* New York: Edward B. Marks Music Corp., 1936.

Gale, Albert, Max Krone, and Beatrice Krone. *Songs and Stories of the American Indians.* Chicago, Ill.: Neil A. Kjos Music Co., 1949.

Graham, Mary Nancy. *50 Songs for Children.* Wisconsin: Whitman Publishing Co., 1964.

Hausman, Ruth L. *Sing and Dance with the Pennsylvania Dutch.* New York: Edward B. Marks Music Corp., 1953.

Kersey, Robert E. *Just Five, A Collection of Pentatonic Songs.* Melville, N.Y.: Belwin Mills, 1972.

Kraus, Richard. *Folk and Square Dances and Singing Games.* Englewood Cliffs, N.J.: Prentice-Hall, Inc., 1966.

Krugman, Lillian D., and Alice J. Ludwig. *Little Calypsos.* New York: Carl Van Roy Co., 1955.

Landeck, Beatrice. *More Songs to Grow On.* New York: Edward B. Marks Music Corp., 1954.

Latchaw, Marjorie, and Jean Pyatt. *Dance Activities.* Englewood Cliffs, N.J.: Prentice-Hall, Inc., 1958.

Lomax, Alan. *The Folk Songs of North America.* New York: Doubleday and Co., 1960.

McConathy, Morgan, Mursell, *et al. Music for Early Childhood.* Morristown, N.J.: Silver Burdett Co., 1952.

Macmahon, Desmond. *Musical Mother Goose.* New York: New Sounds in Modern Music, 1957.

Macmahon, Desmond. *Singing Games.* New York: New Sounds in Modern Music, 1957.

Macmahon, Desmond. *Songtime.* New York: New Sounds in Modern Music, 1957.

Marquis, Margaret Hurley. *Songs for All Seasons* and *Rhymes without Reasons.* New York: Edward B. Marks Music Corp., 1968.

Niles, John Jacob, and Helen Louise Smith. *Folk Ballads for Young Actors* and *Folk Carols for Young Actors.* New York: Holt, Rinehart and Winston, Inc., 1962.

Nordoff, Paul, and Clive Robbins. *The Three Bears.* Bryn Mawr, Pa.: Theodore Presser Co., 1966.

Norman, Ruth. *Action Songs for Growing Up.* New York: Mills Music, Inc., 1959.

Norman, Ruth. *Sing a Song of Action.* New York: Mills Music, Inc., 1950.

Perry, Sylvia, and Lillian D. Drugman. *Song Tales of the West Indies.* Far Rockaway, N.Y.: Carl Van Roy Co., 1964.

Pitcher, Gladys. *Playtime in Song.* New York: M. Witmark and Sons, 1960.

Seeger, Ruth C. *American Folk Songs for Christmas.* New York: Doubleday and Co., 1953.

Seeger, Ruth C. *Animal Folk Songs for Children.* New York: Doubleday and Co., 1950.

Siegmeister, Elie. *Work and Sing.* New York: Edward B. Marks Music Corp., 1944.

Tobitt, Janet E. *Promenade All.* Pleasantville, N.Y.: Box 97, 1947.

Tobitt, Janet E. *The Red Book of Singing Games and Dances from the Americas.* Evanston, Ill.: Summy-Birchard Publishing Co., 1960.

Tobitt, Janet E. *The Yellow Book of Singing Games and Dances from Around the World.* Evanston, Ill.: Summy-Birchard Publishing Co., 1960.

Vanderere, Lilan J. *Far-Away Friends.* Boston, Mass.: C. C. Birchard and Co., 1937.

Wardian, Jeanne F., Helen P. Landsverk. *The New Century Encyclopedia of Song.* New York: Appleton-Century-Crofts, 1971.

White, Florence, and Kazuo Akiyama. *Children's Songs from Japan.* New York: Edward B. Marks Music Corp., 1960.

Zimmerman, George H. *Seasons in Song.* New York: M. Witmark and Sons, 1964.